CW01509260

REPARATIONS

REPARATIONS

Slavery and the tyranny of imaginary guilt

Nigel Biggar

FORUM

FORUM

First published in Great Britain by Forum,
an imprint of Swift Press 2025

9 8 7 6 5 4 3 2 1

Printed and bound in Great Britain by CPI Group (UK) Ltd,
Croydon CRO 4YY

A CIP catalogue record for this book is available from the British Library

We make every effort to make sure our products are safe for the purpose
for which they are intended. Our authorised representative in the EU
for product safety is Easy Access System Europe, Mustamäe tee 50,
10621 Tallinn, Estonia gpsr.requests@easproject.com

ISBN: 9781800755598
eISBN: 9781800755604

To the sailors of the Royal Navy – of all skin colours –
who gave their lives in suppressing the transatlantic
slave trade

CONTENTS

ACKNOWLEDGEMENTS

The following have contributed in a variety of ways to this book, and I thank them now: Robin Baird Smith for first suggesting I write it; Professors Lawrence Goldman, Robert Tombs and François Velde for helping me clarify the slight association of the Queen Anne's Bounty with the slave trade; Professor David Eltis for his critical comments on the second proofs, for confirming his view that the role of slave-trading and slavery in producing Britain's industrial prosperity was 'small' and for explaining the largely indirect nature of his association with the Brattle Report; Rasheed Griffith for giving me a heterodox view from the Caribbean; Justin Marozzi for giving me pre-publication access to the text of *Captives and Companions: A History of Slavery and the Slave Trade in the Islamic World*; Lord (Tony) Sewell, CBE, for referring me to Orlando Patterson's work; and Charles Wide for exposing the gross imprudence of the Church

Commissioners of England in authorising the commitment of £100 million as reparations for the Church of England's profiting from slavery.

This book builds upon some material published elsewhere. I thank the following for their permission to reuse that material: the *National Post*, Policy Exchange, and William Collins.

PREFACE

Guilt, like pain, can be good. When we put our hand next to a flame, it burns and, if our body is functioning well, it hurts. The pain we feel warns us of the physical damage being done and prompts us to pull our hand back. Similarly, the feeling of guilt pains us, alerting us to our having wronged someone and urging us to put things right by apologising and repairing whatever damage we have done. The apology is itself an act of reparation, in that, by communicating to the injured party that we know we have done wrong, we signal that we share their moral view and thereby we begin to restore trust. However, if the wrong we have done is more serious than, say, an unkind word, we need to do more than merely apologise; we need to go further and restore what has been lost or destroyed, or, if that is not possible, offer some equivalent compensation. Guilt as a response to personal wrongdoing is healthy.

But false guilt is not.

In 1976 the Baghdad-born Jewish historian Elie Kedourie published his *In the Anglo-Arab Labyrinth*. In this book he wrote: 'No doubt, great powers do commit great crimes, but a great power is not always and necessarily in the wrong; and the canker of imaginary guilt even the greatest power can ill withstand'.[1]

The guilt he had in mind was the conviction that the British had betrayed the Arabs in permitting Jewish immigration into Palestine after the First World War, since they had promised that Palestine would be part of a new Arab state. Kedourie argues convincingly, I think, that Britain had in fact made no such promise and betrayed no one. Nevertheless, the canker of *imaginary* guilt had come to infect the British Foreign Office, thereby weakening British self-confidence and misshaping British foreign policy.

Today we are again succumbing to a fresh and more general bout of false guilt about our colonial past, which is misshaping the policies of our governments and cultural institutions and weakening our international standing. The 'we' here encompasses all the members of the 'Anglosphere', but especially the British, Australians and Canadians.

This false guilt puts us at the mercy of manipulation by our enemies. For example, when Canada recently sought to launch a UN investigation into China's human rights record regarding its treatment of the Muslim Uyghur people, the

Chinese deflected the attempt by reminding the Canadians of their guilt for the 'colonial' genocide of indigenous children in the Indian Residential Schools.[2] This genocide is now so widely believed in Canada that it has become a public orthodoxy. And yet it never happened. The guilt is entirely false.[3] But because it is believed, it weakens, nonetheless.

Similarly, British guilt over the involvement of some of their ancestors in the enslavement of Africans is also misplaced, as this book will show. But insofar as Britons feel guilty, it makes them vulnerable to exploitation. Almost every chapter of Sir Hilary Beckles's 2013 book-length argument for the British payment of slavery reparations – *Britain's Black Debt* – takes care to open by quoting a member of the (then) recent British Labour cabinet or shadow cabinet. And a campaign in favour of reparations, funded by an Irish billionaire, is now headquartered in the parliamentary office of a Labour MP.

By explaining why the claims of slavery reparations by Beckles and others are false, this book hopes to cure the British of the canker of imaginary guilt at a time when the liberal West needs to keep all its pillars standing confident and strong.

1

INTRODUCTION: WHY NOW?

British involvement in slave-trading and slavery ended 200 years ago, and yet it has become a major public topic in recent years. The reasons are several. The most immediate one was the importation into the UK of the ideology of the Black Lives Matter movement following the killing of George Floyd in May 2020. That has since been exploited by the CARICOM Reparations Commission, which was established in 2013.[1] Yet that in itself is an expression of a wider assertion of the claims of indigenous peoples through the United Nations since the 1960s.

I

Some British people were involved in the trading of African slaves across the Atlantic, and in their enslavement in the Americas, mainly from about 1650 to the early 1800s. In 1807 the British Parliament abolished the trade, and in 1833 the institution, throughout the British Empire. That was almost 200 years ago. Yet British slavery has recently become a major public topic in the UK, and to a lesser extent in Canada and Australia. Why is that?

The immediate cause was the killing of an African American, George Floyd, by a policeman in Minneapolis in May 2020. This fuelled a major upsurge in the US of the Black Lives Matter movement (BLM), which had emerged in 2014 as an informal alliance of people concerned to combat racism in general, and police violence towards black people in particular. The BLM cause quickly crossed the Atlantic, where it was eagerly taken up by anti-racist groups who used it to promote the narrative that the UK, like the US, is systemically racist and that this systemic racism is rooted in historic British slave-trading and slavery. The causal connection between the eighteenth century and the present is 'colonialism', which the British – allegedly – continue to venerate. Therefore, in order to exorcise themselves of racism, the argument goes, the British must repudiate their colonial past, which can be summed up in one word: slavery.

The second cause of the present topicality of British slavery is exploiting the first but is somewhat older. In 2013 CARICOM – the Caribbean Community of fifteen member states and five associates – established a Reparations Commission to press the case for reparatory justice against former European colonial rulers such as Britain for 'native genocide and slavery'. As the Commission's chair, Sir Hilary

Beckles, explained in an address to the House of Commons in the UK Parliament on 16 July 2014,

> One hundred years of colonial oppression followed 250 years of slave trading and chattel slavery. Slavery which ended in 1838 was replaced by a century of racial apartheid, including the denigration of Asian people. The regime of enslavement was crafted by policies and attitudes that were clearly genocidal. Indigenous genocide, African chattel slavery and genocide, and Asian contract slavery, were three acts of a single play – a single process by which the British state forcefully extracted wealth from the Caribbean resulting in its persistent, endemic poverty.[2]

The case for reparations acquired a measure of apparent financial precision with the publication of the 'Brattle Report' in June 2023, which calculated the total debt owed at a conservative us$100–131 trillion and Britain's modest portion of it at over us$26 trillion.[3] Right from the start, Hilary Beckles began pushing the case at the British Labour Party. Each of the fifteen chapters of his 2013 book, *Britain's Black Debt: Reparations for Caribbean Slavery and Native Genocide*, is prefaced with a quotation. One of these is of Jeremy Corbyn, four of Diane Abbott, and two of Dawn Butler – all Labour MPs. Corbyn was Leader of the Labour Opposition from 2015–20, and Abbott and Butler both served in his shadow cabinet. Since then, the lobbying has taken up permanent residence in the UK's Parliament. In March 2023, Clive Lewis, MP, and shadow Foreign Secretary under Corbyn, called for the UK government to enter into 'meaningful negotiations' over reparations with Caribbean countries – supported by Labour MPs Nadia Whittome and Butler.[4] The following autumn, Lewis's parliamentary office became the centre of a campaign in support of reparations, funded by Irish billionaire Denis O'Brien.[5]

The Caribbean claims of reparations since 2013 are one expression of a growing, worldwide assertiveness on the part of formerly colonised indigenous peoples. While this can be traced back to the League of Nations in the 1920s, it began to gather steam through the United Nations in the post-1945 period,[6] finding focus in the 2007 UN Declaration on the Rights of Indigenous Peoples.[7]

II

As the reader will discover later in this book, the simple equation of British colonialism with slavery – which both BLM and the CARICOM Commission make – is historically untenable. Indeed, it is cartoonishly simplistic. Equally, the BLM claim that British society today is systemically racist is empirically untenable.

To begin with, there is the phenomenon that in the last UK government of Boris Johnson in 2019–22, most of the major departments of the British state were headed by Britons of Middle Eastern, Asian or African heritage: Rishi Sunak, Chancellor; Priti Patel, Home Secretary; Sajid Javid, Health Secretary; Nadhim Zahawi, Education Secretary; and Kwasi Kwarteng, Business Secretary. Kemi Badenoch was then Minister of State for Equalities. After Johnson fell from power, the ethnically Indian and religiously Hindu Sunak rose to become Prime Minister. And since Sunak fell, Badenoch, a first-generation black immigrant from Nigeria, has risen to become Leader of the Opposition. If Britain really were systemically racist, that would not have happened – and especially, it would not have happened in a *Conservative* government and in the *Conservative* Party. Racist, white supremacist countries just do not fill the highest offices of state with members of ethnic minorities.

If more comprehensive, social scientific evidence is needed, the 2019 report of the European Union Agency for Fundamental Rights, *Being Black in the EU*, should serve. This found that the prevalence of racist harassment as perceived by people of African descent was lower in the UK than in any of the twelve EU countries surveyed, except Malta. In Finland, the figure was 63 per cent, in Ireland 51 per cent, in both Germany and Italy 48 per cent, and in both Sweden and Denmark 41 per cent. In Britain only 21 per cent of black respondents reported such harassment, the second-lowest result. And the prevalence of overall racial discrimination – in terms of such things as employment, health or housing – was the lowest in the UK bar none. It also found that race relations were worst in Austria and Finland – countries with no history of overseas colonisation.[8]

Then there is the March 2021 'Sewell Report' of the UK government's Commission on Race and Ethnic Disparities (CRED) – eight out of whose nine commissioners were members of ethnic minorities and whose chairman, Dr Tony Sewell, was a Jamaican Briton and descendant of African slaves. This argued that while racism certainly persists in Britain, different socio-economic outcomes for different ethnic groups have a variety of causes, of which racism is only one.[9] As the report says:

> Put simply we no longer see a Britain where the system is deliberately rigged against ethnic minorities. The impediments and disparities do exist, they are varied, and ironically very few of them are directly to do with racism. Too often 'racism' is the catch-all explanation, and can be simply implicitly accepted rather than explicitly examined. The evidence shows that geography, family influence, socio-economic background, culture

and religion have more significant impact on life chanc-
es than the existence of racism ... The evidence reveals
that ours is nevertheless a relatively open society. The
country has come a long way in 50 years and the success
of much of the ethnic minority population in education
and, to a lesser extent, the economy, should be regarded
as a model for other White-majority countries.[10]

The CRED report observes that outcomes vary considerably between different ethnic groups. For example, in
secondary education Chinese and Indian pupils outperform
their white British peers 'by wide margins' in terms of strong
GCSE passes in English and maths. Indeed, when socio-
economic status is controlled for, 'all major ethnic groups
perform better than White British pupils except for Black
Caribbean pupils (with the Pakistani ethnic group at about
the same level)'.[11] And, compared to the US, the attainment
gap between black and white pupils is approximately eight
times smaller.[12] Meanwhile, regarding pay, while Pakistani
Britons earn 16 per cent less on average than their white
counterparts, Bangladeshis 15 per cent less and black Africans
8 per cent less, the white Irish (41 per cent), Chinese (23 per
cent) and Indian (16 per cent) ethnic groups earn more on
average than the white British one.[13] Because of this variety
in outcomes, the CRED report concludes that the divisive

conceptual division of British society into 'White' on the one hand, and 'Black and Minority Ethnic' (BAME) on the other should be abandoned:

> Use of the term BAME, which is frequently used to group all ethnic minorities together, is no longer helpful. It is demeaning to be categorised in relation to what we are not, rather than what we are: British Indian, British Caribbean and so on. The BAME acronym also disguises huge differences in outcomes between ethnic groups. This reductionist idea forces us to think that the principal cause of all disparities must be majority versus minority discrimination ... Like the UK's White population, ethnic minority groups are far from monolithic in their attitudes towards British social norms and their inclusion in different walks of life.[14]

The third set of social scientific data that disturbs BLM's claim that British society today is systemically racist is provided by the World Values Survey 2023. This shows Britain to be one of the least racist countries in the world: only 5 per cent of British respondents objected to having immigrants as neighbours and only 2 per cent to neighbours of a different race – roughly the same as Norway (5 and 3 per cent), Sweden (3 and 1 per cent) and Germany (4 and 3 per cent) and far better than Iran (42 and 28 per cent), Russia (32 and 16 per cent), China (26 and 18 per cent) and Japan (30 and 15 per cent). It is notable that Australia (9 and 4 per cent) and Canada (9 and 4 per cent), both creations of British colonial endeavour, also returned some of the lowest scores.[15]

III

The BLM assumption that contemporary Britain is systemically racist does not square with the presence of members of ethnic minorities in the very highest public offices or with social scientific data, as I have shown. In what follows, I also hope to show that the assumptions of CARICOM's Reparations Commission about British colonialism are wildly distorted and that its case for reparations for historic slavery does not add up.

2

JUDGING THE PAST

The champions of reparations are full of moral indignation against slavery and summarily condemn anyone who had anything to do with it as simply evil. Yet, while we cannot help but judge the past according to our own moral standards, wise judgement will take into careful account the past's very different circumstances, while humble judgement will recognise that our modern common sense is the legacy of a long process of moral enlightenment that our ancestors underwent.

I

Slavery, according to Denis O'Brien, the Irish businessman currently funding a campaign for reparations in the UK's Parliament, was 'a heinous crime'.[1] Indeed, it was so heinous that the British, having perpetrated it, can claim no credit at all for stopping it. Such a fiercely absolute moral judgement lacks any sign of historical awareness. It seems not to know that, until the British made worldwide abolition a major part of their imperial mission, slavery was a universal institution that had existed from the dawn of time. To acknowledge this is not to condone it. As I shall explain in the following chapter, there are good reasons to regard enslavement as morally wrong in principle. But the fact of the universality of slavery should at least excite a measure of curiosity about why so many human beings – of every hue, on every continent – engaged in slavery. And once curiosity has led us to suspend judgement for a moment, so that we make time to understand first, we may find that acquaintance with the circumstances in which our ancestors had to operate will give rise to a modicum of sympathy. Then, when we return to judge, our judgement will be humbled, less puffed up with self-righteous indignation, because it is aware that, had we suffered those circumstances, we might have done likewise. No doubt, we will still judge slavery to be immoral, but without the self-inflating bombast.

II

Why I take this position is, of course, the fruit of my own moral viewpoint. So, before I proceed to explain what I think makes a good judgement about the past, let me first put on the table, face up, the relevant features of my own ethic.

It is shaped, first and foremost, by Christian principles and tradition. That does not mean that readers who are not

Christian need find my moral views entirely alien. After all, before anything else I am a human being, which means that I share a more or less common world with all other humans.

What is more, as a Christian I am inclined to believe that that common world is structured by universal moral principles, to which everyone has access in theory, and my study of ethics, both in the West and outside it, has confirmed that that is indeed so. For example, when, in 2013, I attended a conference on the ethics of war in Hong Kong, I discovered that ancient and medieval Confucian tradition had developed a concept of 'just war' that was very similar to the one developed in the Christian West – in spite of the fact that Chinese civilisation and Christendom had developed almost entirely independently of each other until the early modern period. What they had in common, they had not borrowed from each other. Each in their own way, they arrived at some identical moral conclusions.

My Christian ethical viewpoint involves the belief that there is an objective moral reality that precedes, frames and dignifies with significance all human choices: there are universal moral principles. If that were not so, the Nuremberg Trials were merely victor's vengeance dressed up as justice, and all talk about the moral authority of universal human rights nothing but hot air.

This moral 'realism' includes the belief that all human

beings *really are* basically equal. That bears thinking about, because in so many respects human beings are unequal – in beauty, intelligence, moral virtue, physical strength, material resources, political power, opportunity and, yes, potential. Social engineering can reduce some of those inequalities, but not all of them. I could say that humans are nevertheless equal in 'dignity', but that really would not get us very far, so long as the meaning of 'dignity' remains vague and obscure. The best I can do to clarify it, is to say that I believe all humans share the dignity of being accountable for the spending of their lives to a God who looks with compassion upon their limitations and burdens.

Indeed, I am acutely aware of those limitations of knowledge and power, since I see human beings as creatures, not gods. Frequently, they have to decide and act in the midst of an enveloping fog that blurs the sharpest eyes. Often, they take carefully calculated risks, and still they fail. What is more, they seldom get to write on a clean slate, being fated by the legacy that the past has bequeathed them. When Joseph Chamberlain, British Secretary of State for the Colonies, commented on imperial policy in South Africa in 1900, 'We have to lie on the bed which our predecessors made for us', he spoke with an admirable practical wisdom that academics – including ethicists – and student activists typically lack.[2] Not having such wisdom, they lack a compassionate appreciation of the constraints under which human beings so often have to act. Consequently, they also lack forgiveness for honest error and tragic failure.

Belief in the basic equality of human beings does not imply that all cultures are equal. A culture that can write is superior *in that technical respect* to one that cannot. A culture that knows that the earth is round is superior *in that natural scientific respect* to one that does not. A culture that repudiates slavery is superior *in that moral respect* to one that practises it.

Nor does belief in basic equality mean that social or economic hierarchy is necessarily immoral. Any large-scale human society will need to work out a division of labour, whereby some sit in a planning office while others dig ditches. The moral challenge is to prevent a functional hierarchy, where relations of authority and subordination are justified by organisational efficiency, from ossifying into an essential one, where those relations are thought to be natural.

As for human decisions, actions and policies, their moral rightness or wrongness is not determined simply by their effects or consequences. It matters, for example, not merely that I killed you, but why. Did I intend it, motivated by jealousy or hatred? Did I do it inadvertently, but through culpable negligence? Or was it a complete accident, for which I cannot be blamed? These distinctions are entirely familiar to the law, which distinguishes between manslaughter, homicide and murder. And yet in each case the effect is the same: you are dead.

What decides the moral quality of an act or policy are the motive and intention of the agent, and the proportionality of its means to its ends. Let me explain. To be morally right, a policy must primarily intend or want something good or valuable. Not infrequently, however, circumstances confront us with a dilemma: we cannot achieve one thing that is valuable without (at least the risk of) causing damage to another thing that is also valuable. In such a situation, it might be morally right for us to proceed, knowing that we will probably or even certainly damage the latter. Whether such a choice is morally justifiable depends on the valuable quality of our ultimate goal, but not on that alone. It also requires that the means that might or will cause damage are 'proportionate' – that is, best fitted to achieve the valuable goal, while calibrated to risk minimal damage en route.

The pursuit of what is valuable or good is basic to the moral rightness of anything we do, even if it is not sufficient for it. What is good for us is in our genuine interest. Therefore, there is nothing at all wrong with pursuing our own *genuine* interests – indeed, we have a duty to do so. As with individuals, so with governments. Governments have a responsibility to look after the interests of their people. As the French political philosopher Yves Simon wrote during the Abyssinia crisis of 1935, 'What should we think, truly, about a government that would leave out of its preoccupations the interests of the nation that it governs?'[3] This duty is not unlimited, of course. There cannot be a moral obligation to pursue the interests of one's own people by doing an injustice to others. Still, not every pursuit of national interest does involve injustice; so, the fact that national interests are among the motives for a government's policy need not make it immoral. For example, the fact that Britain's humanitarian policy of suppressing the Atlantic slave trade also benefited British producers of sugar who used free, paid labour in their competition with Brazilian producers who used unpaid, slave labour in no way undermines the morality of the policy.

Sometimes individuals and governments can be well motivated to achieve an important good, and they can choose their means of getting there conscientiously, and yet, through the bad fortune of relentlessly adverse circumstances, *they can still fail*. Not all failure to do good or avoid evil is immoral and culpable. Some of it is honest and tragic. Where that is so, the fitting response is not blame, but lament and compassion.

History contains an ocean of injustice, most of it unremedied and now lying beyond correction in this world. Even with respect to recent crimes, the attempt at human justice is haphazard and its achievement fragmentary. Those sober facts oblige realism about what is possible. Yet human beings seem to have a deep instinct for justice that will not let us settle for less, obliges us to hope against hope and drives us to our knees. The resultant posture, situated between cynicism and utopianism, is well captured by Reinhold Niebuhr's famous prayer: 'God give us grace to accept with serenity the things that cannot be changed, courage to change the things that should be changed, and the wisdom to distinguish the one from the other'.[4]

III

Against moralistic critics of colonialism, it is often protested we ought not to judge the past by the present. That is both true and untrue. It is untrue if it means that we should not judge at all. We are moral beings; we cannot help but make moral judgements and react negatively, say, to historic instances of excessive violence. If we pretend not to judge, we will judge anyway, but obliquely.

On the other hand, it is true that we should not judge the past by the present if it means one of two things. One is that human beings are always in the process of learning morally, and that some moral truths that are obvious to us were just not obvious to our ancestors. To us, for example, it is obvious that slavery is wrong, because it makes one person the absolutely disposable property of another. However, to most of our ancestors up until the second half of the eighteenth century, slavery was a fact of life – an institution that had existed all over the world since time immemorial. There could be good or bad forms of it – some granting slaves certain rights, others not; some being merciful, others being cruel – but the institution itself was taken for granted. We should forgive our ancestors for not perceiving some moral truths quite as clearly as we do, just as we shall surely need forgiveness from our grandchildren for our own moral dullness. Indeed, we should humbly thank our ancestors, since we are the beneficiaries of the legacy of the moral lessons they suffered. What we now take for granted, they had to learn.

The second sense in which it is true that we should not judge the past by the present is that the circumstances of the past were often very different from our own, and that good moral judgements always take circumstances into account. For example, the peace and security that most people in the early twenty-first-century West take for granted as normal are, historically, quite extraordinary. We may hold, for example, to the moral principle that violence should only be used when necessary and kept to a minimum. Yet violence that would be excessive in the peaceful circumstances of contemporary Britain, and in a world governed by the post-1945 international legal order, was not necessarily excessive in the unstable circumstances of weak nineteenth- or early twentieth-century states or in conflicts between peoples representing vastly different cultures and restrained by no commonly recognised conventions. We cannot help but judge the past by our present ethics. We can make sure, however, that our present ethics are informed and moderated by a sensitivity to human limits and frailty and by an historical imagination that enable us to enter sympathetically into the moral constraints and demands of circumstances very different from our own. That is, we can ensure that our morality is not self-righteously, rigidly moralistic.

3

CONTEXT 1: SLAVERY'S UNIVERSALITY

Those calling for Britain to pay reparations like to abstract British involvement in slavery from its historical context, so as to make it seem uniquely abhorrent. Part of that context is the fact that slave-trading and slavery were universal institutions, practised in a variety of forms by people of every skin colour on every continent since ancient times. Difficult though it may be for us, we need to exercise our imaginations to step out of our own world and back into that of the past, in order to understand why.

I

Denis O'Brien's view that slavery is 'a heinous crime' is now commonplace. We in the early twenty-first-century West naturally view slavery as abhorrent and we struggle – if we bother to struggle at all – to understand how anybody in the past could have associated themselves with it. We instinctively regard slave traders and slave masters with horror and angry indignation as incomprehensively evil people. 'How *could* they have done such things?', we ask.

That is a fair question. But before we ask it, we need to pause and consider two things: first of all, what we mean by 'slavery'; and second, the fact of its universality.

II

Historically, slavery has come in a variety of forms. It varied both in the nature of the relationship between slave and master and in its legal status. Therefore, I suggest, it also varied in its moral quality. Even if we think all slavery bad, it was not always equally bad.

One of the obvious features of slavery we regard as evil is hard labour. Yet many kinds of work are laborious, physically exhausting and soul-destroyingly tedious, without quite amounting to enslavement. Think, at least, of contemporary construction workers and fruit-pickers. Think, further, of rural labourers, miners or canal diggers before the age of mechanisation, whose work was often back-breaking, sometimes lethal. Most people in the past earned their daily crust by means of hard, physical labour sustained over long hours, which the typical reader of this page would find utterly intolerable.

In one sense, these people were forced to work in this way, because, under the conditions of the time, including limited technological development, sheer survival required it. Yet the conditions of life often force things upon us that we would rather not do. Often that is not unjust; it is merely unfortunate. And those of us privileged to live in present times and places of unprecedented health, wealth and security are much more fortunate than most of our ancestors.

Other kinds of coercion, however, may be unjust. Often, labour performed under the terms of an 'indenture' has been considered unfairly coerced. So, for example, when, at the turn of the nineteenth century in the aftermath of the Second Anglo-Boer War, the British government authorised the recruitment in China of labourers for work in the gold mines of South Africa's Witwatersrand, the liberal political philosophers L.T. Hobhouse and Gilbert Murray condemned it as de facto slavery.[1]

The immediate reason for the decision was to save the mining industry, which faced a 66 per cent shortfall in labour.[2] But upon that industry depended the post-war recovery of the economy, and upon that recovery depended the post-war peace in South Africa. In addition, Lord Milner, then governor of the Transvaal and the Orange River Colony, was concerned to pre-empt an alliance of Boers and British mine-owners demanding that Africans be subjected to *truly* forced labour.

Accordingly, between 1904 and 1906 over 63,000 Chinese were recruited in China for work in South Africa.[3] But they were recruited, not forced. They voluntarily signed contracts, otherwise known as 'indentures', which obliged the subscriber to work for three years' duration and stated the working hours, the nature of the work, the rate of wages, the rations and the right to free medical attendance. Recruiting agents were obliged to make sure that recruits fully understood the terms to which they were subscribing, and a superintendent was appointed to run an administration to look after the interests of the labourers in South Africa.[4] Liberal metropolitan indignation was overheated: this was no 'Chinese slavery'. And when, in 1906, the new Liberal government sought to end the use of indentured labour from China by offering to fund early repatriation, 'few opted to return voluntarily'.[5]

Nor was this form of labour confined to people with non-white skins. It had originally been used to attract young, able-bodied men to work overseas for a period, in the hope of escaping poverty at home and setting up a better life abroad. Between 1650 and 1780, 50–66 per cent of Europeans migrating to North America did so under contracts of indentured servitude.[6] The terms and conditions of their indentures varied, but they would commonly involve an agreement to work for a specified number of years without pay (to discharge a debt) or for a fixed wage, in return for free transport to a colony, board and lodging, and perhaps the opportunity to settle. It was only in the later nineteenth and early twentieth centuries that the British Empire sought to make up for local shortages of labour by authorising the recruitment of indentured labourers from Asia, mainly India.

Indentured servitude was not a form of slavery. It was not forced but contracted. It lasted only for a limited period and it gave the subscriber certain rights. No doubt, the terms were often harsh and the contracts unfair. The conditions of life and work were certainly very poor: from 1719–58 European indentured servants newly arrived in Jamaica died at four times the rate of newly arrived Africans of the same age, with 36 per cent of all indentured servants dying within five years.[7] Still, such severity, injustice and tragedy do not amount to slavery.[8]

III

What distinguishes and specifies slavery as the simple evil that we now understand it to be is not hard labour, legal compulsion or an unfair contract. What specifies it is that the slave's time and employment are owned, not voluntarily under certain conditions for certain purposes and for a certain length of time, but absolutely. The slave is the slave-owner's disposable property, to be put to whatever use the owner decides, and to be bought and sold – and perhaps even killed – at will. That is the pure form or paradigm of slavery, and it is the treatment of another human being as absolutely disposable property that makes it categorically worse than other forms of unjust employment.[9]

Nevertheless, it is important to remember that, historically, not everything that went by the name of 'slavery' fitted this simply evil form. In different times and places the condition of the slave differed. Imagine the following scene. It is the 1500s and we are visiting a well-off home in Mecca. Our host sits drinking tea. Suddenly, he flies into a rage, shouting at a young man who is leaning down to speak to him, and hits him with a fly swatter. Another, slightly older, man rushes over and receives some instructions, together with some gold coins. Pointing to the man he has just smacked, our host exclaims, 'This disappointment. I know he wishes for my death!' Then, turning to the other man he has instructed, he adds, warmly, 'But you pray for my long life'. Curious to know who the two men are, we discreetly ask the older one. He tells us that his name is Saffron and that he has worked in this house for five years. In a year's time, however, he will have saved enough money to move out and start his own business. What about the younger man? 'Oh, that poor boy', says Saffron, 'he'll be here till the old man dies'. The abused young man, it turns out, is our wealthy host's son. Saffron, on the other hand, authorised to act for his master in business matters, is a trusted slave. And he is in the process of buying back his freedom by instalments.[10]

So, 'slavery' has not always lived down to our grim assumptions. Sometimes slaves have in fact been better off than contracted employees or even their master's own children. Indeed, sometimes they have risen to positions of considerable wealth and power. From 1555 to 1579, for example, Sokullu Meḥmed Pasha was grand vizier (or prime minister) of the Ottoman Empire during the reign of three sultans. He was married to a sultan's daughter and owned thousands of slaves. And yet he was himself a slave.[11]

Sometimes there were legal or customary constraints on what owners were permitted to do with their human property: the right to ownership was not always absolute. For example, an owner was sometimes forbidden to strike or kill his slave, or obliged to grant them their freedom, under certain conditions. And where a failure of proprietorial duty was liable to incur legal penalties, and where those penalties were applied, there slaves had an enforceable right. Yet even where there were no legal constraints and no corresponding rights, slave-owners whose consciences retained a measure of sensitivity may have felt morally obliged to use their legal freedom humanely – say, by not selling a male slave apart from his wife and children, if they could possibly avoid it.

However, when all the qualifications have been duly made, it remains the case that where slaves were radically dependent upon the will of their master for their livelihoods, their families, and even their lives, and where that will was subject to little or no effective legal constraint, the institution of slavery was highly objectionable. For even if it did happen to occasion decent treatment, it did not secure it, leaving slaves infinitely vulnerable and fearful. And, at the worst, it permitted the most dreadful abuse.

IV

Slavery was not only various in form, but ancient in origin. In order to understand why this was so, we need to exercise our historical imaginations and leave behind the world around us that we take so for granted. In peacetime today, we have elaborate prison systems into which we can put dangerous criminals, sometimes for decades, in order to keep the rest of society safe from them. These penal systems are very expensive, and, if they were to offer better conditions of life than they currently do, they would be a lot more expensive than they are.

Similarly in wartime, we are now obliged under international law to take enemy combatants who have surrendered and confine them in prisons under sufficiently humane conditions. This, too, is expensive.

In the past, however, our ancestors were not so wealthy. They could not afford to incarcerate defeated enemies in large numbers for a long period of time. And when they did, the conditions of incarceration were often inhumane. Take, for a notorious example, the Confederate prisoner-of-war camp at Andersonville during the American Civil War of 1860–65. Almost 30 per cent of the 45,000 soldiers held there died, because the Confederate government lacked the resources to provide adequate housing, food, clothing or medical care.[12] Consequently, for much of history all over the world, when one people defeated another in battle, they often slaughtered the defeated troops – since that was the only way of ensuring that they did not return to fight them again.

Enslavement was an alternative to slaughter. As David Eltis has written, 'the substitution of slavery for death … legitimated slavery throughout history'.[13] Therefore, however counter-intuitive it may seem to us and however difficult to swallow it might be, enslavement sometimes represented a measure of moral progress. As the late nineteenth-century moral philosopher David Ritchie put it, slavery was

a necessary step in the progress of humanity … [since] [i]t mitigated the horrors of primitive warfare, and thus gave some scope for the growth, however feeble, of kindlier sentiments towards the alien and the weak …

Thus slavery made possible the growth of the very ideas which in course of time came to make slavery appear wrong. Slavery seems to us horrible ... It used not to seem horrible.[14]

V

Not only was slavery ancient; it was universal. Across the globe societies employed slave labour in agriculture, mining, public works and even as troops. All the ancient Mesopotamian civilisations practised slavery in one form or another, starting with Egypt in the third millennium BC. To the west, around the shores of the Mediterranean Sea, the ancient Greeks, Carthaginians and Romans followed. To the east, slavery could be found among the Chinese from at least the seventh century AD, and subsequently among the Japanese and Koreans. In the Americas, the peoples of the Pacific North-West practised it from before the sixth century AD,[15] the Incas and the Aztecs extracted forced labour from subject peoples from the fifteenth century, and the Comanches 'built the largest slave economy' in what is now the south-west of the US from the eighteenth century.[16]

From the time of Muhammad in the 600s onward, slavery was practised throughout the Islamic world. In the eighth and ninth centuries the Vikings supplied markets in Arab Spain and

Egypt with slaves – again, *white* slaves – from eastern Europe and the British Isles. In the 1600s corsairs or pirates from the Barbary Coast of North Africa raided English merchant ships, and even villages in Cornwall and west Cork, for slaves. One estimate has it that raiders from Tunis, Algiers and Tripoli alone enslaved between 1 million and 1.25 million Europeans from the beginning of the sixteenth century to the middle of the eighteenth century.[17] Another estimate reckons that the Muslim slave trade as a whole, which lasted until 1920, transported about 17 million slaves, mostly African, exceeding by a considerable margin the approximately 11 million shipped by Europeans across the Atlantic.[18] As Justin Marozzi has written,

> it was Africa which bore the brunt of the Islamic world's insatiable demand for slave labour. Slavers plied its Mediterranean, Atlantic and Indian Ocean coasts, traders raided inland for human cargo, and millions of enslaved Africans trudged across the Sahara into captivity. Meanwhile, North African corsairs turned the Mediterranean into a slaving free-for-all between Muslims, Christians and Jews ... Sanctioned by the Prophet Mohammed, legitimated by the Quran and holy law, slavery endured for fifteen centuries. Abolition had few champions and came late in the day – hereditary slavery even continues in Mali and Mauritania.[19]

VI

This is a basic part of the context of European involvement in the trading and enslavement of black Africans from the mid-fifteenth century onwards. Current discussion of slavery and reparations, however, prefers to ignore it altogether. It does so in order to pretend that the British enslavement of blacks was something extraordinary and that it was the origin of the white-versus-black racism that infects British and other anglophone societies today.

In fact, as I have shown, slave-trading and enslavement were universal practices, carried out by people of every skin colour on every continent. Africans were busy enslaving other Africans and selling them to the Romans and Arabs centuries before British merchant ships appeared off the coast of West Africa in the mid-1600s. The British were by no means unique culprits.

4

BRITISH SLAVERY

Over a century and a half of slave-trading and slavery undoubtedly profited Britain. But how great the profit was is a highly controversial question. The claim that it was 'enormous' and that Britain's industrial prosperity was 'founded' on it is not widely accepted by economic historians. Most reckon slavery's contribution to have been modest, at best.

I

Like most other peoples throughout history, the English were involved in slave-trading from early on. During the Anglo-Saxon period, Bristol was a major centre for selling (white) people enslaved in Wales or the north of England to the Vikings, who exported them across to Dublin, up to Scandinavia, down the Volga, and into the Black Sea and the Muslim world. However, lobbying by Wulfstan, Bishop of Worcester, and Lanfranc, Archbishop of Canterbury, persuaded William the Conqueror to shut down the Anglo-Irish trade in the eleventh century.[1] And by the thirteenth century, slavery in general had lost all legal status in England and northern France.[2]

II

Meanwhile, in West Africa, Africans were being enslaved by other Africans, before being sold to Arab traders and exported to Muslim lands around the Mediterranean and in Arabia. Slavery and the slave trade, then, had been alive and well in Africa long before European merchants arrived on the coast in the fifteenth century. The Portuguese were the first to seek slaves from West Africa in the 1440s, to make up for a labour shortage in Portugal and to man sugar plantations on their island possessions in the Atlantic, not least Madeira. Between 1525 and 1866 the Portuguese Empire is reckoned to have shipped 5,841,468 slaves out of Africa, amounting to 46.7 per cent of the total of African slave exports of 12,508,381. After the Portuguese came the English – or, from 1707, the British – with 3,259,443 slaves exported, or 26.1 per cent of the total, mostly between 1640 and 1807.[3] The exporting was primarily done by merchants operating under the charter of the Royal African Company, which was founded in 1672.[4]

The conditions under which slaves were transported across the Atlantic were infamously dreadful, with the human cargo tightly packed below decks, initially shackled, starved of daily fresh air and sunlight for all but an hour or two, malnourished, dehydrated and prey to disease for a voyage lasting up to six weeks. One African witness, Olaudah Equiano, who survived the ordeal in the mid-1750s, described it thus:

> The stench of the hold ... now that the whole ship's cargo were confined together ... became absolutely pestilential. The closeness of the place, and the heat of the climate, added to the number in the ship, which was so crowded that each of us had scarcely room to turn himself, almost suffocated us. This produced copious perspirations, so that the air soon became unfit for respiration, from a variety of loathsome smells, and brought on a sickness among the slaves, of which many died ... This wretched situation was again aggravated by the galling of the chains, now become insupportable; and the filth of the necessary tubs [latrine buckets], into which the children often fell, and were almost suffocated. The shrieks of the women, and the groans of the dying, rendered the whole a scene of horror almost inconceivable.[5]

General mortality statistics lay bare the scale of the suffering. According to one estimate, of the African slaves shipped by British traders in 1672–87 a full 23 per cent were 'lost in transit'.[6]

Most of those who survived the sea journey were deposited in the Caribbean, especially Barbados and Jamaica. Some were taken beyond to the coast of the American colonies, mostly south of New Jersey. There they were sold at auction as pieces of property or 'chattels', often separated from their families.[7] In the West Indies and southern American colonies they were put to work on plantations, probably producing sugar, though perhaps tobacco or rice. Organised into regimented gangs, they were subject to severe discipline, which was too often cruel. In 1654 a French priest, Antoine Biet, reported how one master in Barbados whipped a slave 'until he was all covered in blood', and then 'cut off one of his ears, had it roasted, and forced him to eat it'.[8] In 1680 an English clergyman berated Barbadian planters for inflicting on their slaves punishments such as castration, amputation and 'even Dissecting them alive'.[9] Punishment for rebellion could be even more sadistic. In 1675 after a failed slave revolt, several of the ringleaders were executed by being burned alive.[10] In 1741 the leader of the 'Great Negro Plot' in New York City suffered the same dreadful fate.[11] And in 1763 runaway slaves who were supposed to have confessed to the murder of two whites were burned alive 'by a slow fire behind the Court House' at Savanna-la-Mar in Jamaica.[12]

The treatment of slaves was not always so horrific. Sometimes masters regarded them with a certain benevolence as members of their extended household, taking a kindly interest in their lives. Sometimes slaves were manumitted, usually by paying an agreed price, less often by getting baptised or being granted freedom in their master's last will and testament.

Nonetheless, slaves remained radically dependent on their master's will and accordingly vulnerable. Because slavery had not had any legal status in England for centuries, the common law was completely silent on the status and treatment of slaves. Thus, the colonies were left free to formulate their own codes, which typically gave owners almost complete control over the movements of their slaves, whose company they kept and how they behaved. Unlike indentured servants, they 'effectively had no legal redress against maltreatment'.[13]

Further, the conditions of work were very harsh, especially on the sugar plantations. Slaves commonly toiled for their owners for up to twelve hours a day, six days a week, without pay. They were malnourished, labouring in a very debilitating climate and prey to a wide array of diseases. Unsurprisingly, they suffered a high rate of mortality. As a result, before the ending of the slave trade, none of the sugar colonies in the West Indies managed to achieve a natural increase in the slave population. That is why they had to keep on bringing in fresh supplies of slaves.

III

While slavery in the sugar plantations of the West Indies was often among the most cruelly oppressive, the use of slaves on a massive scale for hard labour on plantations was neither invented by Europeans in the Caribbean nor confined to it. As Mohammed Bashir Salau asserts, 'plantations were not peculiar to the Americas'.[14] In the nineteenth century they were established by Omani Arabs on the coast of East Africa,[15] and by the Fulani in the Sokoto Caliphate in what is now northern Nigeria. Indeed, the Caliphate became 'one of the largest slave societies in modern history',[16] equalling the United States in the number of its enslaved (4 million).[17]

Nonetheless, can it be claimed that the suffering of slaves on ships crossing the Atlantic or cutting cane in the British West Indies was unique in its brutality?[18] In the sixteenth century, children, often African, destined to serve as eunuchs in charge of the royal harem in the Ottoman palace were forcibly castrated. This involved using a cord to tighten the penis, scrotum and testes together, slicing them off with a razor, applying boiling oil to stop the bleeding, and inserting a lead nail into the urethra to stop it contracting.[19] And of the plight of a white European slave of an Arab master on the Barbary Coast of North Africa, Robert C. Davis has written (quoting Henri-David de Grammont): 'as chattel of whomsoever chose to buy him, he would be utterly without rights or a will of his own, his very life forfeit to the whim of his new owner, who "could resell him, overload him with work, imprison him, beat him, mutilate him, kill him, without anyone interfering"'.[20] The experience of Miguel de Cervantes, who was captured and enslaved in 1575, bears this out. According to a first-hand witness, Cervantes 'was on the verge of losing it [his life] on four different occasions when he was nearly impaled or hooked or burned alive because he had sought to liberate many others ... In the end, [his accomplice] the gardener was hung by a foot and died by drowning in his own blood.'[21]

Was it worse to be subjected to punishment by bodily mutilation as a plantation slave than to be castrated for service as a eunuch? Or was it worse to be burned alive as an African plantation slave in Barbados than as a European galley slave on the Barbary Coast? Not obviously.

Perhaps one might try to estimate quantities of suffering by enslavement and then compare them. Approximately 12.5 million Africans were enslaved by Europeans from 1501 to 1875, amounting to 33,333 per annum. Of these, about 3.26 million were enslaved by the British from 1551 to 1807, amounting to 12,684 per annum.[22] This compares to a conjectured 17 million enslaved first by Africans and then sold to Arabs from, say, 700 to 1900, amounting to a mere 14,166 per annum. However, to put all this in proportion, let us recall that the Nazis murdered about 6 million Jews in the four-year period of 1941–5, amounting to 1.5 million per annum.

Still, can we say that transatlantic slavery involved a greater aggregate quantity of suffering than its Arab counterpart? Not really. Human suffering is only as great as an individual human being can experience it.

IV

Famously, in his seminal *Capitalism and Slavery* (1944), the Trinidadian historian (and, later, Prime Minister) Eric Williams argued that profits from the slave trade provided a major source of capital for financing Britain's world-leading industrial revolution and made 'an enormous contribution to Britain's industrial development'.[23] His thesis has been controversial ever since. Williams himself was quite clear in not claiming that the slave trade was 'solely and entirely responsible for industrial development'.[24] So the controversy has concerned its effect relative to other factors.

In the late 1960s Roger Anstey minimised the slave trade's effect by calculating that its profits fell far below Williams's estimate and could not have financed the industrial revolution to a significant extent.[25] Anstey's general view has been confirmed more recently by David Richardson, who estimated that profits from the slave trade probably contributed

45

under 1 per cent of total domestic investment around 1790.[26] Arguing in the same direction, David Eltis and Stanley L. Engerman have shown that the slave trade engaged only 1.5 per cent of British vessels and 3 per cent of tonnage. On this they comment that if

> economic activity on so modest a scale could contribute significantly to industrialization, then we might expect Europe's first industrial economy to have been Portugal, not Britain. Though Portugal had less than one-third the population of Britain in the late eighteenth century and a total national income which was no doubt still lesser, the country's nationals nevertheless managed to carry nearly two-thirds again as many slaves across the Atlantic than did the British over the course of the slave-trade era.[27]

In 2010, David Brion Davis, the distinguished historian of slavery and its abolition in the Western world, confidently pronounced the last rites on Williams's thesis, declaring that it 'has now been wholly discredited by other scholars'.[28]

The slave trade is one thing; however, slavery itself is another. Some argue that, of all economic sectors, the Atlantic slave-based economy – especially sugar production – made the most significant contribution to Britain's industrial development.[29] But Eltis and Engerman are highly sceptical: 'Sugar was just one of hundreds of industries in a complex economy', they write; 'and while sugar was one of the larger industries, its linkages with the rest of the economy and its role as an "engine" of economic growth compare poorly with textiles, coal, iron ore, and those British agricultural activities which provided significant inputs to industry'.[30] Another economic historian, Joel Mokyr, agrees: 'In the absence of West Indian slavery, Britain would have had to drink bitter tea, but it still would have had an Industrial Revolution, if perhaps at a marginally slower pace'.[31]

Nevertheless, the slave economies of British colonies did serve to fuel the growth of external trade and thereby generate the accumulation of further capital. The growing demand for sugar on the part of British consumers stimulated increased production in the West Indies, which in turn stimulated the importation of clothing and equipment from Britain and slaves from Africa. Kenneth Morgan comments:

> The growth in English exports supplied to the Americas in the mid-eighteenth century helped to expand production in the textile, metal, and hardware industries in Britain. The need to provide such export goods at an accelerating rate may well have aided the diffusion of technical innovation, notably in cotton spinning, to the British textile industry. And so it is likely that the main

stimulus of the slave trade to the British economy lay in the channels of increasing demand. It would be incorrect to claim that the wealth flowing home from the slave trade was a major stimulus for industrialization in Britain, but it would not be unfair to claim that the slave-sugar complex strengthened the British economy and played a significant, though not decisive part, in its evolution.[32]

Significant, not decisive.

V

The most recent interventions in the debate about the economic effects of the slave trade and slavery have been made by Maxine Berg and Pat Hudson in their book, *Slavery, Capitalism, and the Industrial Revolution* (2023) and David Eltis in *Atlantic Cataclysm: Rethinking the Atlantic Slave Trades* (2024).

On the one hand, Berg and Hudson in effect confirm that critics of Williams have been correct to deny his claim that Britain had emancipated slaves in 1833 only when the sugar economy of the West Indies was no longer profitable. '[T]he sugar trade continued to boom right through the eighteenth and into the early nineteenth century, remaining strong and profitable' up to and beyond 1833, they write, and 'between 1807 and the abolition of preferential sugar import duties for

British colonies in 1846 ... planter and mercantile fortunes continued to be made from Caribbean business'.[33]

However, they do argue that 'the role of slavery in the process of industrialization and economic transformation ... has been generally underestimated by historians ... Slavery, directly or indirectly, set in motion innovations in manufacturing, agriculture ... shipping, banking, international trade, finance and investment, insurance ...'.[34] Yet, the word 'indirectly' signals the vagueness of the claim and the difficulty of substantiating it. They muster few examples of close causal connections between slavery and industrialisation. This is not surprising, because the capitalist economy of landholding, banking and merchanting was largely separate from the industrial economy of small provincial entrepreneurs, who developed local enterprises based on capital networks involving only their own kin and co-religionists. They tended to be nonconformist Protestants committed to slavery's abolition.[35]

Moreover, some connections that Berg and Hudson try to make strain credulity. For example, their claim that the slave-based economy of the Atlantic was bound up with the wider economy of the Indian Ocean 'rests unsteadily on one product, Indian textiles', according to Tirthankar Roy.[36] Further, they suggest that the costs to the British state of using the Royal Navy to protect overseas trade – and of fighting very expensive wars with the likes of France to do so – were an overall benefit, since 'spending on the navy . . . stimulated the economy'.[37] Yet, they provide no analysis that shows that such naval and military spending was outweighed by the commercial profits.

In fact, while arguing that the economic stimulus of slavery was more widespread than is supposed, Berg and Hudson are very cautious in what they claim: 'We do not argue that slavery caused the industrial revolution', they write. 'Neither do we suggest that slavery was necessary for the development of industrial capitalism in Britain.' And, while they do at one point tentatively suggest that incomes earned from the transatlantic slave economy accounted for 'perhaps . . . around 11%' of GDP at the end of the eighteenth century,[38] they disclaim any 'attempt to estimate that the gains from slavery contributed a particular percentage of Britain's economic growth, GDP or capital formation in the eighteenth century, as earlier studies have attempted . . . many aspects of the impact of slavery are not measurable in quantitative terms'.[39] Such modesty falls a long way short of endorsing Williams's claim of slavery's 'enormous' contribution to Britain's industrial prosperity.[40]

Nonetheless, David Eltis is unequivocal in his criticism.[41] Of Berg and Hudson's book, he comments that it

does not use TSTD [the Trans-Atlantic Slave Trade database] correctly and offers arguments that the slavevoyages data do not support ... The body of the text is a 216-page catalogue of what reads like all possible connections between individual slave traders and their businesses on the one hand, and the economy that lay beyond the slave trade on the other ... their book has a startling lack of analysis ... Even though Britain never had the largest slave empire and even though the Iberian powers clearly did, but never showed traces of industrialisation, the authors are certain that their long list of descriptive links between the slave sector and the rest of the economy is evidence of slavery triggering accelerating economic growth first in Britain.[42]

In this, Berg and Hudson are typical of 'the new historians of capitalism, the authors of the 1619 project, most scholars of the slave trade, and all the media [who] frequently distort the history of slavery by greatly exaggerating its economic importance.'[43] To all those who 'see slavery as the foundation of quickening growth in the metropole', Eltis puts the Portuguese case:

For more than three centuries Portugal was the leading Atlantic slave trader and, at least until 1825 when Brazil became independent, the possessor of the largest single source of plantation produce in the early modern

Atlantic world . . . [Yet] 'by the middle of the nineteenth century Portugal became one of the most backward economies of Europe' . . . Today, Portugal is the poorest country in the EU, despite Portuguese pre-eminence in the Atlantic slave trades.[44]

On the argument that slavery was the basis of British economic prosperity, Eltis comments, 'How very odd that such a small proportion of slaves and their owners that were British (1.7 per cent of the enslaved global population . . .) should have triggered an Industrial Revolution.'[45] Then, setting irony aside, he speaks forthrightly: it is 'beyond credulity that slavery or the slave trade that supported it could have kick-started economic growth. It is far more likely that the key to such development lay in conditions within Britain . . .'.[46]

VI

There is no doubt that a century and a half of trading in slaves and employing slave labour profited some Britons directly and many others indirectly. Exactly how much it contributed to GDP is uncertain. That said, not even Berg and Hudson agree with Eric Williams that it made an 'enormous' contribution. Kenneth Morgan reckons it 'significant', but less than 'decisive'. And David Eltis – described by Henry Louis Gates,

Jr, as 'the world's leading scholar of the slave trade' – thinks that is overstating it.[47] Regarding the significance of the slave trade to the economy of slaving ports such as Liverpool, he writes of its 'triviality'.[48]

It is no doubt true, as Berg and Hudson argue, that slavery generated profits and technological advances whose benefits have ramified down the centuries to the present day. It follows that more of Britain's present prosperity is 'tainted' by slavery than meets the eye. But so it is by the unjust exploitation of nameless medieval serfs and Victorian industrial workers. And so it is around the world, not least in West Africa. The truth is that little of what anyone, anywhere inherits is untainted by some historic wrongdoing or other. We cannot scrub out the stain. All we can do is strive to use our tainted inheritance better.

5

CONTEXT 2: AFRICAN COMPLICITY

Advocates of British reparations for slavery invariably downplay African complicity in slave-trading. But Africans had been enslaving and selling other Africans since Roman times. Europeans merely furnished them with a new, if larger, market.

I

The universality of slavery is one of the contexts that advocates for reparations like to downplay. African complicity in European slave-trading is another, which they strive to overlook altogether. Thus, Michael Banner reports vaguely that the slaves bought by British merchants 'had been captured in war or simply kidnapped', without identifying who was doing the raiding and kidnapping, namely Africans.[1] Hilary Beckles goes even further, asserting that African chiefs generally resisted the slave trade.[2]

In support of this view, the sixteenth-century, militantly Catholic King Afonso I of Kongo is often invoked.[3] In particular, reference is made to these passages extracted from two letters written by Afonso to King John III of Portugal in 1526. The first is dated 6 July:

> Each day the traders are kidnapping our people – children of this country, sons of our nobles and vassals, even people of our own family. This corruption and depravity are so widespread that our land is entirely depopulated. We need in this kingdom only priests and schoolteachers, and no merchandise, unless it is wine and flour for Mass. It is our wish that this Kingdom not be a place for the trade or transport of slaves.

The second is dated 18 October:

> Many of our subjects eagerly lust after Portuguese merchandise that your subjects have brought into our domains. To satisfy this inordinate appetite, they seize many of our black free subjects ... They sell them. After having taken these prisoners [to the coast] secretly or at night ... As soon as the captives are in the hands of white men they are branded with a red-hot iron.[4]

The existence and nature of slavery and slave-trading in Africa before European demand for slaves came into play was a matter of controversy among historians in the last four decades of the twentieth century.[5] However, against those who argue that European demand changed 'a less intensive or non-existent slave system to a more exploitative one aimed at foreign commerce', John Thornton's close study of Afonso's correspondence with Portugal has shown 'that Kongo probably did have a well-developed system of legal slavery at the time of its first contact with Portugal, and that the trade in slaves was always acceptable under Kongolese law'.[6] Contrary to appearances, Afonso's letters in 1526 are not protesting against slave-trading as such. Rather, they are complaining about the subversion of its regulation. In the earliest extant letter, dated 15 October 1514, Afonso regularly mentions both gifts of slaves – referred to, dehumanisingly, as 'pieces' – and the possibility of them being purchased in Kongo.[7] In the letter of 18 October 1526, he complains, not about Portuguese slave-raiding, but about Kongolese nobles breaking the royal monopoly of the slave trade and enslaving and selling Kongolese freemen, thereby undermining royal control:[8] 'As long as it was his army conducting his wars that captured slaves, and as long as enslaved people were being sold on royally supervised markets, he was content with the institution'.[9] In general, writes Thornton, 'Central African rulers controlled states typical of their era throughout the world ... Holding people as slaves ... [was] part and parcel of this larger system of government.'[10] And not just hold-ing; also selling on a considerable scale: five or six years after Afonso's death, a Portuguese witness testified at an inquest that Kongo was exporting overseas between 4000 and 8000 slaves per annum.[11] Writing in 2009, Linda Heywood agrees, unequivocally: 'Slavery as an institution existed from the time that Kongo emerged as the dominant power in West Central Africa in the fourteenth century' and the kingdom of Kongo 'consistently exported large numbers of slaves throughout the period of the trade [the 1500s to the 1800s]'.[12]

At the end of that period, when the British Empire began to commit itself to promoting the abolition of slavery and slave-trading, African rulers resisted. According to the Beninese historian Abiola Félix Iroko, '[w]hen the slave trade was abolished [by the British], Africans were against abolition. King Kosoko of Lagos was against abolition at the time ... Of those who were sold and had offspring ... [s]ome returned home ... [and] became, in turn, slaveholders and bought slaves for their correspondents who remained in Brazil. Africans resumed this trade after abolition.'[13] John Iliffe, Professor of African History at Cambridge University, concurs, writing that '[m]any African leaders resisted the abolition of the slave trade. Kings of Asante, Dahomey, and Lunda all warned that unsold captives and criminals would have to be executed.'[14]

Hilary Beckles's claim is false.

II

While the treatment of slaves in transit across the Atlantic and in the plantations of the Americas was usually brutal, there was at least one fate suffered by African slaves of African masters that slaves of European masters did not undergo: human sacrifice. Africans had been enslaving other Africans for centuries, mostly by capturing them in war or raids, sometimes taking them in lieu of debt. Often slaves were destined for profitable export, first to Roman markets, then to Arab ones, and finally to European ones. But they also had their local uses, which included supplying victims for human sacrifices.

The practice of human sacrifice in West Africa was attested as early as the tenth century by Ibn Hawqal,[15] and by Europeans 400 years later. Human sacrifices – as distinct from the judicial execution of criminals – served a variety of purposes: sometimes to appease the gods, but more often to supply a deceased master with servants in the afterlife, to make a conspicuous display of extravagant wealth, and to intimidate onlookers. Although wives, favourites, women and foreigners were also liable to serve as victims, slaves – usually war captives – were the main source. Commonly, their fate, especially at funerals, was to be buried alive. One report in 1797 has it that between 1400 and 1500 people were sacrificed at royal funerals in Asante.[16]

III

As the effects of colonial slavery upon Britain are controversial, so are its effects on Africa. And they are likely to remain so, since data on trends in output and population in pre-colonial Africa are scarce. Some argue that the Atlantic slave trade made little difference to most of Africa, though it might have had a greater impact on the population and wealth of societies along its Atlantic coast.[17] Others hold that it had devastating consequences, causing widespread depopulation and economic dislocation, undermining the socio-political fabric of African societies, and propagating forms of slavery and servitude hitherto unknown.[18]

Although it is impossible to calculate the costs to Africa of the slave trade with any precision, it makes sense to suppose that British (and European) demand for slaves stimulated African endeavour to supply – and thereby an increase in war and slave-raiding in West and Central Africa. While the British investors and merchants bear responsibility for that, so do their African suppliers. Commercial and political elites in West and Central Africa 'appear to have made large profits from helping to meet the American demand for slave labour'.[19]

Moreover, to those inclined to see Africans as the helpless victims of the European demand for slave labour, the late eighteenth-century Dahomean ruler, King Kpengla, offers a strong rebuttal. In response to English abolitionist suggestions that Dahomey only made wars to capture slaves for the European market, he observed that whereas England was protected by sea, his country was in the middle of a continent and surrounded by enemies. Consequently, Dahomey was

> obliged, by the sharpness of our swords, to defend ourselves from their incursions, and to punish the depredations they make upon us ... your countrymen, therefore, who allege that we go to war for the purpose of supplying your ships with slaves are grossly mistaken ... if white men chose to remain at home ... will black men cease to make war? I answer by no means.[20]

6

CONTEXT 3: BRITISH ABOLITION

The British were among the first peoples in the history of the world to abolish slave-trading and slavery. They did not do it because the slave plantations in the West Indies were becoming unprofitable, nor primarily because of slave uprisings. They did it principally because of the growing humanitarian conviction, largely Christian, that one human being owning another as his absolute property is immoral.

I

The British were actively involved in the transatlantic slave trade for about 150 years until 1807, and in employing slave labour for almost three decades beyond that, until 1834. Slavery had lost its legal status in England itself in the thirteenth century, as was confirmed, in effect, by the judgement of Lord Mansfield in the case of *Somerset v Stewart* in 1772.[1] In Britain's colonies in the Americas, however, slavery was widely accepted. This was so much the case that even the 'maroons' – runaway slaves who hid out in the forested interiors of Jamaica and elsewhere – kept slaves of their own. What is more, they were prepared to secure their own autonomy in 1739 by agreeing to stop freeing slaves, to return escaped slaves to their owners and to assist white settlers in suppressing slave revolts.[2] Mavis Campbell comments:

> it is certain that the Maroons did keep slaves among themselves, though not on a large scale to be sure. Now what is to be said of a people who fought their way successfully out of slavery, just to turn around and to commence slaving others? Without attempting a moralistic reply, we can only remind ourselves that in almost all known slave societies, from antiquity to modern, slaves have been known to keep slaves. Furthermore, in most slave revolts – Spartacus's being the most outstanding – the rebels' aim was invariably to reverse the system and not to overthrow slavery as such.[3]

Four years after his own manumission at the age of 35, Toussaint Louverture, later the famous black leader of Haiti's successful slave revolt, owned at least one slave and rented a coffee plantation with thirteen slaves for two years in 1779–81.[4]

Nevertheless, in the second half of the eighteenth century both the slave trade and the institution of slavery came under mounting public criticism in Britain. Why this occurred when and where it did is an interesting question. The answer is probably a combination of humanitarian ideas, increased awareness of African enslavement, and the prospect of being able to doing something about it.[5] Two main intellectual streams fuelled the opposition. One was a body of Enlightenment philosophers, which included the French Baron de Montesquieu and the Scottish Adam Smith.[6] In his highly influential *De l'esprit des lois* (1748, translated into English two years later), the former objected to slavery because of its demoralising effects on both parties: by robbing slaves of their freedom, it makes it impossible for them to act 'through a motive of virtue', and because 'by having an unlimited authority over his slaves [the master] insensibly accustoms himself to the want of all moral virtues, and from thence becomes fierce, hasty, severe, choleric, voluptuous, and cruel'.[7] Smith went further, romanticising Africans in his *Theory of Moral Sentiments* (1759) and attributing to the slave a superior moral dignity:

There is not a Negro from the coast of Africa who does not . . . possess a degree of magnanimity which the soul of his sordid master is too often scarce capable of receiving. Fortune never exerted more cruelly her empire over mankind than when she subjected those [African] nations of heroes to the refuse of the gaols of Europe, to wretches who possess the virtues neither of the countries which they come from, nor of those which they go to, and whose levity, brutality, and baseness, so justly expose them to the contempt of the vanquished.[8]

Whereas Enlightenment philosophers influenced the literate, educated elite, the inspiration of the extraordinarily popular movement to abolish the slave trade and slavery in the late eighteenth century was Christian. Anti-slavery sentiment flourished widely among English Dissenters or Nonconformists – especially the Quakers – and the Methodist or evangelical wing of the Church of England. John Wesley, Anglican priest and founder of Methodism, prefaced his *Thoughts Upon Slavery* (1774) with a quotation from the Bible: 'And the Lord said – What hast thou done? The voice of thy brother's blood crieth unto me from the ground' (Genesis 4:10). The context is Cain's murder of his brother Abel and the implication is clear: African and Englishman, slave and master, are brothers, common children of the same God. In what follows Wesley counters the argument that slavery rescues Africans from an even worse plight, by presenting evidence, first, of the prosperity, culture and high social organisation of West African peoples, and then of the barbaric treatment meted out to them as slaves by their English masters. As he draws to a close, Wesley addresses readers who have inherited slaves:

Perhaps you will say, 'I do not *buy* any negroes: I only *use* those left me by my father'. – So far is well; but is it enough to satisfy your own conscience? Had your father, have *you*, has any man living, a right to use another as a slave? . . . It cannot be, that either war, or contract, can give any man such a property in another as he has in sheep and oxen. Much less is it possible, that any child of man, should ever be *born a slave*. Liberty is the right of every human creature, as soon as he breathes the vital air. And no human law can deprive him of that right, which he derives from the law of nature.

If therefore you have any regard to justice, (to say nothing of mercy, nor of the revealed law of GOD) render unto all their due. Give liberty to whom liberty is due, that is to every child of man, to every partaker of human nature. Let none serve you but by his own act and deed, by his own voluntary choice. – Away with all whips, all chains, all compulsion! Be gentle towards men. And see that you invariably do unto every one, as you would he should do unto *you*.[9]

Anti-slavery sentiment acquired practical, political focus in 1787 with the founding of the Society for the Abolition of the Slave Trade in London. Among its founding members

was Thomas Clarkson, who promoted the sale of the autobi-
ography of Olaudah Equiano, a former slave whom we met in
Chapter 4,[10] and who collaborated with William Wilberforce
and other members of the Clapham Sect in mounting and
sustaining a campaign both inside and outside Parliament.[11]
Extra-parliamentary agitation was considerable: in 1791
about 30 per cent of the adult male population of Britain
signed anti-slavery petitions.[12] Events overseas also played
an important part in shaping public opinion at home. The
1791 rebellion of slaves in Saint-Domingue, which neither the
French nor the British could suppress and which culminated
in the foundation of the independent, black-led Republic of
Haiti in 1804, helped to give abolition the appearance of historical inevitability. Nonetheless, let it be noted, the rebellion
took place *after* the abolitionist Society had been established.
The British campaign for abolition preceded it.

The efforts of the campaigners finally bore fruit in 1807,
when Parliament legislated to abolish the slave trade. It took
a further 26 years to achieve the Empire-wide abolition of
the institution of slavery itself, initially because the leading
abolitionists were politically conservative and assumed that
cutting off fresh supplies of slaves would doom the slave-
based economies to wither naturally, gradually and with
minimal disruption. Even most black abolitionists were grad-
ualists until the 1820s.[13]

However, when the plantations proved more resilient than had been expected, agitation to hasten abolition picked up steam. In an attempt to slow things down, the government presented the colonial legislatures with proposals to ameliorate the condition of the slaves in 1823. These included granting the right to present evidence in court, removing hindrances to manumission, establishing savings banks for slaves and imposing legal restrictions on punishments. Yet whereas the government's proposals could bind the Crown colonies, they could not oblige the older ones such as Barbados and Jamaica, which enjoyed the right to self-government and had their own legislative assemblies. There London's efforts at amelioration ran into fierce resistance.[14]

Given the recent experience of the American War of Independence in 1776–83, subsequent British governments can be forgiven, I think, for being reluctant to override colonial assemblies. If they pressed too hard, they risked the permanent loss of humanitarian influence. So, when urged to legislate for the likes of Jamaica in 1824, George Canning, Foreign Secretary, responded: 'no feeling of wounded pride, no motive of questionable expediency, nothing short of real and demonstrable necessity, shall induce me to moot the awful question of the transcendental power of parliament over every dependency of the British Crown. That transcendental power . . . ought to be kept back . . . It exists, but it should be veiled.'[15]

Still, colonial recalcitrance was one factor in converting many cautious, conservative minds to the cause of immediate abolition. Another was the savage retribution meted out to black rebels (and their white missionary supporters) in the slave revolts in Demerara in 1823 and Jamaica in 1831–2. In July 1832, Lord Howick, Under-Secretary of State for the Colonies, wrote to the new Governor of Jamaica: 'The present state of things cannot go on much longer ... Emancipation alone will effectually avert the danger.'[16] The following year Parliament passed the Slavery Abolition Act, which came into effect twelve months later. Thus, on 1 August 1834, slaves throughout the British Empire were formally emancipated.

II

In recent times the greatest controversy attending the abolition of the slave trade and of slavery itself has stemmed from a further thesis proposed by Eric Williams. In *Capitalism and Slavery* (1944) not only did Williams hold that profits from the trade had financed Britain's industrial revolution; he also argued that the trade and the institution had been abolished because they were no longer profitable.

This second thesis has been quite as contentious as the first. Against Williams, Roger Anstey demonstrated in 1975 that, in terms of economic interest, 1806–7 was the worst possible time for Britain to abolish its slave trade, embroiled as it was in a long war with Napoleon.[17] Two years later Seymour Drescher published *Econocide: British Slavery in the Era of Abolition* (1977), which presented a mass of empirical evidence that abolition amounted to an act of suicide for a major part of Britain's economy.[18] Drescher showed that the value of trade between the West Indies and Britain had increased sharply from the early 1780s to the end of the eighteenth century, and that the West Indies' share of total British overseas trade did not enter long-term decline until well after the flow of fresh supplies of slave labour had been cut off by Parliament. What is more, as we noted in Chapter 4, even Maxine Berg and Pat Hudson concur.

Therefore, while Williams continues to have his supporters, it is fair to say that the weight of judgement among contemporary historians falls heavily against him.[19]

III

Further controversy over the process of abolition has concerned the agreement to compensate slave-owners for their loss of property to the tune of £20 million, which was paid by the government and funded by metropolitan taxpayers. That concession is controversial today and it was controversial then.

The government was already committed to abolition, but it preferred to win the consent of the West Indian planters rather than coerce them. The shadow of the French Revolution and its Terror was long and made unthinkable the idea of the state riding roughshod over the right to property. The payment of compensation to the slave-owners was considered a distasteful but necessary political compromise. The Anti-Slavery Society, which had been founded by Wilberforce and Clarkson in 1823, was not happy with many aspects of the Slavery Abolition bill, but they supported it rather than jeopardise the momentum towards emancipation. Clarkson was quite unapologetic about the compensation, viewing it 'not as an indemnification but as money well paid for procuring the cooperation of the West India Planters and Legislators, without which the abolition of slavery might have been materially obstructed and retarded, if not prevented'.[20]

The decision to compensate the slave-owners in 1833 is often used by 'decolonisers' to discredit the abolition movement today, as Williams's thesis sought to discredit it in 1944. There is no denying that it was a political compromise, but peaceful politics usually requires compromise, and some compromises are morally justified, even obligatory.

Besides, the planters claimed that they faced ruin without compensation and, given the (to them) novel, additional cost of paying wages to previously slave labour, that claim is plausible. Even with compensation, many planters sold up within twenty years of emancipation, which suggests that their business model was indeed precarious. In 1834, for example, there were 670 sugar plantations in Jamaica; by 1854 that number had dropped by over half to 330.[21] From this it is reasonable to infer that, without compensation in 1833, at least some plantations would have gone bankrupt, with the consequent loss of employment opportunities for those free slaves who, for one reason or another, could not find land of their own on which to subsist – especially on Antigua and Barbados. Many ex-slaves chose to stay working on plantations after the end of mandatory apprenticeship, because of the housing, medical care and food provided.

IV

Yet, that period of apprenticeship has also been controversial. Vital to the argument for reparations, as the Anglican ethicist Michael Banner makes it, is the downplaying of the significance of the British abolition of the slave trade and slavery. The title of the relevant sub-section of his book makes his thesis crystal clear: 'Abolition: a.k.a. the Continuation of Servitude'.[22] 'What we [British] celebrate as the ending of years of gross and flagrant injustice and unfreedom', he writes, 'was followed by years of gross and flagrant injustice and freedom … Britain did not turn over a new leaf at emancipation, but found new ways of unjustly extracting value from its colonies, right down to modern times.'[23] One of the targets in Banner's sights here is the fixed period of the post-emancipation 'apprenticeship' of freed slaves from 1834–8, which, he complains, was 'a form of tied labour'.[24]

That is undoubtedly true. Upon formal emancipation on 1 August 1834, all slaves over the age of six were required to become apprenticed labourers, paid for overtime, but bound to perform unpaid work for their former masters for between 40 and 45 hours a week for a transitional period of up to four years for domestic slaves and six years for field slaves, after which they would be fully emancipated. The rationale for this was to give the plantations time to adjust and survive economically. This was in the interest not only of the owners but also of those freed slaves who would not be able to find land of their own on which to subsist and who therefore would depend on the plantations for employment.

Although special imperial magistrates were appointed to supervise the system and ensure fair play, they were too few, too underpaid and too weak vis-à-vis the colonial assemblies to be effective. The result was that planters were able to hinder black apprentices from developing economic independence and to continue exploiting their labour. However, revived abolitionist agitation in Britain, combined with signs of unrest among apprentices, persuaded the government to end the transitional system two years early, on 31 July 1838. In Jamaica, Trinidad and British Guiana, many emancipated slaves found unsettled land on which to subsist, but in smaller colonies such as Antigua and Barbados, where free land was not readily available, employment on the plantations remained the only option.

V

Against Banner's claim that the emancipation of slaves in 1834 was purely formal and made no material difference at all stands the record of the Codrington plantations on Barbados, which had been bequeathed to a legally autonomous missionary body associated with the Church of England, the Society for the Propagation of the Gospel (SPG), in 1710.

From the beginning, the treatment of slaves during the SPG's ownership was comparatively less brutal, and as time went on it became progressively more humane, especially in anticipation of emancipation. The proposal in 1711 to instruct slaves in the Christian religion, which was opposed by other planters, implied a certain trans-racial equality.[25] In 1732, an SPG attorney, the Rev. Arthur Holt, wrote to the London owners in indignant protest against the branding of slaves: 'these letters SOCIETY in large Characters are Brandished with a Red hot Iron upon the naked Breast of the New Negroes as If they were So many Beasts, a Cruelty which I believe the Society will think proper to Discourage'. Shortly afterwards, without waiting for a response, Holt unilaterally ordered the branding stopped.[26]

From 1760 the SPG underwent 'a profound change in ... outlook and policy' and moved towards the idea that it should 'uplift and reform him [the African slave] for a full share in Christian civilization'.[27] It became increasingly committed to promote both the physical and spiritual welfare of slaves and there is evidence that its humanitarian example influenced other plantations.[28] In 1767 the slave's customary right to own property and spend money was recognised.[29] In 1792 two new hospitals were commissioned and the burden of field work was reduced.[30] In 1795 schools were established for the education of black children, and in 1823 'an extraordinarily ambitious and expensive program of education' was launched.[31] According to the historian J. Harry Bennett, by 1823 'the Codrington blacks were treated with unusual humanity' and from 1825 the SPG's African slaves 'were the beneficiaries of an eminently progressive policy in their schools, church, and villages'.[32]

When the prospect of the formal abolition of slavery appeared on the horizon, the SPG committed itself to gradual emancipation from 1831: the whipping of female slaves was abolished; writing and arithmetic were taught in schools;

the sale of slaves was stopped; freedom from enforced labour was made purchasable; a savings bank was set up; and an allotment system was established, giving each slave family a cottage and a plot of land.[33] During the apprenticeship period from 1834, the freed slaves were entitled by law to their customary provisions of food, clothing and medical care from the plantations, they were paid for overtime work, and they were able to grow crops for sale as well as subsistence.[34]

To claim, as Banner does, that nothing changed for the better in the run up to, or aftermath of, emancipation in 1834 is to obscure the subtler truth. As Kenneth Morgan puts it, 1838 marked 'the birth of a free peasantry throughout the British West Indies'. By 1846 freed blacks in Jamaica, aided by Baptist missionaries and British philanthropists, had acquired nearly 100,000 acres by purchase alone and had built nearly 200 free villages.[35] That may not have been everything; but it was a lot more than nothing.

VI

Banner disagrees, however: 'The end of enslavement did nothing materially for a population the value of whose labour had been appropriated – misappropriated – for generations'.[36] Plantation-owners maintained patterns of work 'little better than slavery'[37] and merely subjected free slaves 'to new forms of servitude and impoverishment'.[38] Unfavourable regulations governed contracts and restrictions on freedom of movement inhibited free bargaining for wages.[39] And the importation of cheap labour in the form of indentured servants from India kept wages low.[40] As a consequence, many black West Indians opted to emigrate, especially in the economic depression of the 1880s, which Banner describes as 'a rather drastic expression of agency and protest'.[41]

Historians beg to differ. B.W. Higman confirms Morgan's claim, writing that in Jamaica, where the size of the island meant that land was readily available, there occurred after emancipation the rapid creation of a 'new class of black smallholders', who were largely independent of labouring for a wage.[42] And the influential Codrington plantations provide evidence of an instance of the creation of a savings bank, to encourage free labourers to accumulate capital.

As for unfair contracts, constraints on wage-bargaining, and emigration – while lamentable, they would all have been perfectly familiar to rural and industrial workers in Victorian Britain. The condition of workers in the West Indies after emancipation was, by our privileged, twenty-first-century Western standards, very poor indeed. But so it was for most people all over the world, regardless of the colour of their skins.

7

CONTEXT 4: BRITISH ANTI-SLAVERY

After abolishing the trade and the institution throughout their empire, the British used their imperial power to suppress slavery worldwide from Brazil to New Zealand for a century and a half. Advocates for reparations routinely ignore this.

I

Advocates of reparations for slavery typically downplay the moral achievement of abolition, claiming that it was inspired by the black-led revolution in Saint-Domingue or that it only occurred because the slave system had become uneconomic, or complaining that slave-owners received compensation, but not slaves. Britain's subsequent century and a half of worldwide suppression of slavery, they ignore absolutely.

The neglected story is this.

Abolitionist ardour in Britain did not grow cold after Parliament had been persuaded to abolish the slave trade and slavery within the British Empire. It went on to move the imperial government to adopt a permanent policy of trying to suppress both the trade and the institution worldwide. One sign of this enduring commitment was the emergence in the Foreign Office of a separate Slave Trade Department from 1819, which was in fact the Office's largest department in the 1820s and 1830s.[1] During the Congress of Vienna in 1814–15 Britain used its diplomatic clout to try to secure support for a general abolition treaty between all the major European powers, albeit in vain. Before and after the congress, however, it did succeed in getting nearly all the states still involved in the Atlantic slave trade to agree in principle to end it – including Portugal, Spain, France, Brazil and the United States. None, however, would consent to a reciprocal right of search of suspect shipping, which was required to give practical bite to the principle. Nevertheless, the British government persisted to such an extent that in 1842 the Foreign Secretary, Lord Aberdeen, saw fit to describe anti-slavery diplomacy as a 'new and vast branch of international relations'.[2]

The British deployed diplomacy, but also hard power. Up to ten ships of the Royal Navy were stationed off the coast of West Africa to disrupt the export of slaves until 1833. Over the next ten years their number rose as high as 19, and from 1844 to 1865 it seldom fell below 20, for several consecutive years stayed at over 30, and twice reached a peak of 36. At its height, the West African station employed 13.1 per cent of the Royal Navy's total manpower.[3] From 1839 naval patrols extended south of the equator, and in 1845 the Slave Trade Act authorised the Navy to intercept Brazilian ships suspected of carrying slaves, to arrest those responsible and to have them tried in British admiralty courts. In 1850 Navy ships began trespassing into Brazilian territorial waters to accost slave ships, sometimes even entering its harbours and on one occasion exchanging fire with a fort. In September of that year Brazil yielded to the pressure, enacted legislation comprehensively outlawing the slave trade and began to enforce it rigorously. Shortly before his death in 1865 Lord Palmerston, twice Prime Minister, wrote that 'the achievement which I look back on with the greatest and purest pleasure was forcing the Brazilians to give up their slave trade'.[4]

Meanwhile, on the eastern side of the mid-Atlantic, the British employed a variety of means to achieve the same end. The thesis of Sir Thomas Fowell Buxton – proposed in his 1839 book *The African Slave Trade and Its Remedy*[5] – that the key to ending the slave trade and slavery in Africa was to promote alternative, 'legitimate' commerce had found wide acceptance. This led to the setting up of trading posts in West Africa, and then, when the merchants complained of the lack of security, a more assertive colonial presence on land.[6] The year after strong-arming Brazil, the British attacked Lagos and destroyed its slaving facilities, having tried in vain to persuade its ruler to terminate the commerce in slaves. In 1861, when an attempt was made to revive the trade, they annexed Lagos as a colony.

On the other side of the continent the British brought persistent diplomatic pressure to bear upon the Sultanate of Zanzibar, which was the main port for the Great Lakes slave trade, but which also depended on the Royal Navy to protect its shipping from pirates in the Indian Ocean. Treaties were signed banning trade in slaves to the Americas in 1822 and to the more important Persian Gulf in 1845. In 1873 the Sultan gave way when Sir Bartle Frere, Governor of Bombay and a resolute opponent of the East African slave trade, threatened a naval blockade unless the export of slaves from the African mainland ceased altogether and the slave market was shut down once and for all. Bit by bit the trade in slaves was throttled. The institution of domestic slavery, however, was tolerated until Zanzibar became a British protectorate in 1890. Between then and 1909 a series of measures gradually emancipated slaves, first of all granting them rights against maltreatment and of self-redemption, then adding a right to obtain freedom on application to the courts. Here, too, slave-owners were compensated for their loss, partly in recognition that domestic slavery was sanctioned by Islamic law, but also to minimise the economic disturbance and political opposition.[7]

The humanitarian motive to suppress the slave trade and slavery remained a common reason – if rarely the only one

– for imperial endeavour in Africa from the late nineteenth century into the twentieth. It caused the British government to lean upon the Khedive of Egypt to sign the Anglo-Egyptian Slave Trade Convention in 1877. It propelled General Charles Gordon into the Sudan in the same year. It found expression in the principles of the Imperial British East Africa Company, when it was founded in 1888. It featured among the reasons for establishing a British protectorate in Nyasaland in 1891. And it was one reason for the invasion of the Sokoto Caliphate (now northern Nigeria) by Frederick Lugard in 1903.

Imperial intentions to stop the slave trade in the Atlantic and Indian oceans were comparatively easy to realise through the Royal Navy's command of the seas. Success in suppressing the trade across the African mainland was more difficult to achieve, because it required the control of large swathes of territory. The elimination of the practice of slavery was also difficult, because it often involved interfering with a long-established and deeply embedded social institution, hallowed by custom, and legitimated by law and religion. Therefore, it risked causing major economic disruption, provoking fierce political opposition and having to compel compliance with resources that were usually very limited. For those reasons, some officials in the East India Company opposed action against slavery in India.[8] Notwithstanding this, the Company eventually passed the Indian Slavery Act in 1843, which forbade officers in the discharge of their public duties from being involved in the trading of slaves or from enforcing rights of property in slaves, and which granted slaves the right to own property and equality under the penal law. Eighteen years later, the Indian Penal Code of 1860 proceeded to make the enslavement and trading of persons criminal offences.[9]

Further east in what is now Malaysia and Indonesia, however, the company was much bolder. Shortly after the Slave Trade Act was passed in 1807, in the person of Sir Stamford Raffles it summarily abolished the importation of slaves and slavery itself on the island of Penang. Subsequently, Raffles banned slave importation in Java, and in 1818–19 he emancipated the slaves in Bencoolen and established a school for their children.[10]

II

As the passing of the Slavery Abolition Act of 1833 had required the compensation of slave-owners, so subsequent attempts by the British Empire to suppress slavery often involved political compromise. However powerful the Empire was, it was not all-powerful: it did not have the resources to send ships or troops to every part of the globe, in order to impose its will. And even when it did send troops, it sometimes came off worst. Notoriously, in 1842 a British army of 4500 (plus 12,000 camp followers) was annihilated in its retreat from Afghanistan.

In 1879 1300 British and colonial troops were overwhelmed by Zulu warriors at Isandlwana in South Africa. And in 1883 an 8000-strong Anglo-Egyptian army was annihilated at El Obeid in the Sudan by the forces of the Mahdi, the purported redeemer of Islam. In this last case, the suppression of the slave trade was among the grievances of the Mahdists.[11]

Lacking the power always to impose, the Empire often had to act against slavery by increments, being careful not to excite too much opposition. Basil Cave, who was Consul-General in Zanzibar when domestic slavery was finally abolished in 1909, bore witness to this when he reflected with satisfaction on the local history of British efforts at abolition:

> all the time British influence was being steadily brought to bear upon the Sultan ... Whenever an opportunity presented itself, when the Sultan appealed for political, financial, or personal assistance, when some benefit was offered or conferred ... occasion was always taken to introduce some fresh anti-slavery measure and to move one more step forward towards final abolition.[12]

As a result, 'the whole of the servile population of East Africa has been freed from bondage without a hand, and almost without a voice, being raised in protest'.[13]

The desire to avoid provoking political opposition was not

the only reason for moving gradually: there was also the recognition that the practice of domestic slavery in the Islamic
world was generally not as inhumane as the plantation slavery of the West Indies. As Lord Cromer, the British reformer
of Egyptian government from 1877 to 1907, put it, domestic
slavery could command 'mitigating pleas', which, while not
justifying its existence, should 'temper the zeal of the reformer who aspires towards its immediate abolition'. He believed
that, as a general rule, slaves in Egypt were well treated, and
'it may be doubted whether in the majority of cases the lot of
slaves in Egypt is, in its material aspects, harder than, or even
as hard as that of many domestic servants in Europe'. Indeed,
whereas the latter could be thrown out of employment at
any moment, '[c]ustom, based on religious law, obliges [an
Egyptian master] to support his slave', if the latter chose not
to emancipate herself. Besides, almost all the slaves in Egypt
were women, and when they left the harems, they had no
means of supporting themselves. Therefore, to have summarily abolished the legal status of slavery would have been 'in the
highest degree imprudent'.[14] And imprudence is a moral vice.

III

The task of estimating the cost of *all* the Empire's various
efforts to abolish the slave trade and slavery at sea and on

land, worldwide, over the course of a century and a half, would present – at the very least – a major challenge both in scale and in complexity. No one, to my knowledge, has tried it. Some, however, have developed an estimate of the expense of transatlantic suppression alone. David Eltis reckoned that this cost British taxpayers a *minimum* of £250,000 per annum – which equates to £1.367–1.74 billion, or 9.1–11.5 per cent of the UK's expenditure on development aid, in 2019 – for half a century.[15] Moreover, in absolute terms, the British spent almost as much on suppressing the trade in the 47 years of the peak period, 1816–62, as they received in profits over the same length of time leading up to 1807. And by any more reasonable assessment of profits and direct costs, Eltis reckons, the nineteenth-century costs of suppression were certainly bigger than the eighteenth-century benefits.[16]

Chaim Kaufmann and Robert Pape took a broader view. In addition to the costs of naval suppression, they considered the loss of business caused by abolition to British manufacturers, shippers, merchants and bankers who dealt with the West Indies. They also factored in the higher prices paid by British consumers for sugar, since duties were imposed to protect free-grown British sugar from competition by foreign producers who continued to benefit from unpaid slave labour. Overall, they 'estimate the economic cost to British metropolitan society of the anti-slave-trade effort at roughly

1.8 per cent of national income over sixty years from 1808 to 1867'.[17] Although the comparisons are not exact, they do illuminate: in 2021 the UK spent 0.5 per cent of GDP on international aid and just over 2 per cent on national defence. Kaufmann and Pape conclude that Britain's effort to suppress the Atlantic slave trade – *alone* – in 1807–67 was 'the most expensive example [of costly international moral action] recorded in modern history'.[18]

8

THE POST-COLONIAL CARIBBEAN

Those promoting reparations claim that relatively poor socio-economic outcomes in former British colonies in the Caribbean are caused by historic enslavement. However, the causal connections are more asserted than demonstrated, the outcomes vary quite dramatically among the former colonies, and authoritative voices argue that they have more to do with post-colonial mismanagement.

I

Advocates for reparations talk up the continuity between the past and the present, asserting that historic slavery two centuries ago is the cause of disadvantages suffered by the descendants of slaves today. In addition to denying the positive effects of formal emancipation, this assertion also involves exaggerating the economic delinquencies of colonial government. Thus, writes Michael Banner, 'The central continuity' between the periods of slavery and emancipation 'is that colonial power continued to be exercised in the interests of the metropole, white elites, and British capital, and with little regard to the interests of the colonies and their people ... Britain conceived no future for the Caribbean except as a source of cheap raw materials, and as a market for British products.'[1]

The relationship between Britain and its Caribbean colonies was 'governed throughout by what Hilary Beckles terms "extractive colonialism"'.[2] The imperial government in London and the colonial governments in the West Indies failed to take up their responsibilities for education and economic development until the very eve of the end of colonial rule, and industrialisation was never entertained as a major objective.[3] As CARICOM's 'Ten-Point Reparation Plan' comments, 'For 400 years the trade and production policies of Europe can be summed up in the British slogan: "not a nail is to be made in the colonies"'.[4] Consequently, Britain's Caribbean colonies, having embarked upon independence in the 1960s with chronic underinvestment, remain to this day 'persistently and relatively poor', their governments burdened by debt and relying heavily on tourism.[5]

However, CARICOM, Beckles and Banner are quite wrong about colonial economics in general. The neo-Marxist theory they adopt tends to come off worse when confronted with the data.[6] Rudolf von Albertini, whose work was based 'on exhaustive examination of the literature on most parts of the colonial world to 1940' (according to the eminent imperial economic historian David Fieldhouse), judged 'that colonial economics cannot be understood through concepts such as plunder economics and exploitation'.[7] And CARICOM's wild claim that the imperial British were resolved to suppress the development of industrial production in their colonies hardly squares with facts such as that the Tata Group, which now owns what remains of the steel industry in Britain, was established by English-educated Indian entrepreneurs in Bombay in 1868 and went on to set up both cotton mills and iron and steel factories under the Raj. The global market of ideas and goods that was the British Empire gave opportunities, not just to British investors, but also to native entrepreneurs.

It is true that, for most of their history, colonial governments did not usually direct the economic development of their colonies. That is because, like most governments until the twentieth century, the public goods they served were mainly the maintenance of internal law and order and external defence. Government in general was small. Up until 1914, British government spending during peacetime was only about 8 per cent of GDP; US government spending, about 3 per cent.[8] It was the experience of beneficial state control of the economy during the two world wars that ushered in the era of much bigger, more widely interventionist government. (By 2022, the figures for the UK and the US had risen, respectively, to 44 per cent and 36 per cent.[9]) Nonetheless, by establishing the rule of law and sufficiently stable government, even small colonial government indirectly encouraged private investment. The leading exporter of capital from the mid-nineteenth century to at least 1929, Britain invested over a third of its overseas capital in the Empire between 1865 and 1914.[10] While 70 per cent of that went to the white-settled colonies or dominions, a not-insubstantial 19.29 per cent was directed to India and a further 10.48 per cent to 'dependent colonies' such as those in the West Indies.[11] Of course, British investment often profited British investors, but it also built infrastructure, exported expertise, and created jobs in the colonies.

Where there was limited external investment before 1939, it was not because of a deliberate policy of keeping the native populations down. Rather, it was partly because investing in tropical agriculture was generally unattractive and investing in industrial production outside the mining industries of Southern and Central Africa was often unprofitable, since limited colonial markets favoured importation rather than local manufacture, especially during the long period (from the 1840s to the 1930s) when faith in the free market militated against protection.[12] This faith was abandoned when a combination of the effects of the First World War, demands from the settler dominions for a system of imperial preference, and the Great Depression moved the British Empire to adopt a policy of imperial protectionism from 1932 to the early 1950s. The results were mixed. Colonial consumers, of course, sometimes lost out. But colonies producing luxury goods such as sugar benefited. Indeed, according to Fieldhouse, imperial preference 'saved the West Indies . . . from disaster'.[13]

II

In addition, the imperial government did begin to shoulder responsibility for direct development, starting with the Colonial Development Act 1929, which made available modest funds for capital schemes such as the building of an infrastructure of public utilities.[14] Eleven years later, the Colonial Development and Welfare Act 1940 authorised expenditure of up to £5 million per annum on colonial development and welfare for a ten-year period and £500,000 for colonial research annually without term. (£5 million in 1940 equates to £358 million, and £500,000 to £36 million, today.) Unfortunately, wartime exigences prevented implementation.[15] At the war's end, a much more generous Colonial Development and Welfare Act 1945 increased the funding available to £120 million (or £6.6 billion today) over a ten-year period.[16]

As for education, it is true that, until very late, the main providers were missionaries, not colonial government.

Nevertheless, after the government of all the West Indian colonies (except Barbados) had been taken out of the hands of planter-dominated assemblies and into the hands of the Crown by the mid-1870s, 'more money [was] devoted to education'.[17] And by the late 1930s a black and brown middle class had 'emerged mainly as a result of the system of public education . . . since the late nineteenth century'.[18]

Given all this, it is not true to say that British colonial governments in the nineteenth and early twentieth centuries did nothing towards the economic development of the West Indies. They did play a role in development, initially indirect, latterly direct. But did they *under*develop? To answer that question, we first need to know what measure is being applied – what the correct level of development is supposed to have been and how 'correctness' is being determined. Neither CARICOM, nor Beckles, nor Banner tells us.

III

Beckles claims, and Banner echoes him, that colonial governments did the Caribbean no economic good at all and left the West Indian colonies completely unprepared to stand on their own economic feet after formal independence in the 1960s. But Tirthankar Roy, the West Bengali-born Professor of Economic History at the London School of Economics and co-author of *The Economic History of Colonialism*, strongly disagrees:[19]

> The claim that Caribbean states were not able to 'find their feet' at independence around 1962 is total rubbish. Jamaica, Trinidad and Tobago, and Barbados had the highest average income and literacy rates in the region, incomes per head were three to four times that in the long-independent Dominican Republic and Haiti, literacy rates were around 15 [per cent] in Haiti and 75–80 [per cent] in Jamaica. Almost certainly, public health was also similarly advanced.[20]

As for the causes of the present economic woes of Britain's former colonies in the West Indies, Roy has this to say:

> Jamaica after independence was particularly badly governed and saw a deep stagnation between 1972 and 1984, when standards of living actually fell. There are few countries in the world not engaged in civil war that had as bad a growth record as did post-independence Jamaica. Average income recovered only so much that its real average income is now what it had been around 1975. Overall, the West Indies region saw rather little economic growth in the 1970s, 1980s, 1990s, when many

Asian countries (colonial or not) forged ahead. The reason was bad and corrupt government, not the burden of colonialism.[21]

The economic history of Barbados since 1945, as told by DeLisle Worrell, former governor of the nation's central bank, confirms this:

Barbados was transformed from an economy based on export agriculture with poor human development in 1945, to one based on tourism, with an HDI score that puts the country in the top category of human development. Although gains have continued to be made in the years since Independence in 1966, the essential transformation was achieved in the 1950s and 1960s.[22]

Since Barbados only became independent in 1966, most of this economic development occurred in the late, post-war colonial period. So, what went wrong afterwards?

Government budgeting was characterised as prudent in the early years of Independence, and the public services demonstrated relatively high productivity. Government savings contributed one-third of capital spending over the period from 1945 to 1980. In stark contrast, the public sector was described in 2016 as overstaffed, poorly skilled and with low productivity. The relaxation of fiscal discipline from the mid-1980s resulted in a balance of payments crisis which required deep economic contraction in 1991, and that pattern was repeated from 2013 to 2018, with another balance of payments crisis in that year.[23]

Between decolonisation in the 1960s and 1970s and the present, many causal factors other than the legacy of colonial government have come into play. Those include the agency of the members of independent Caribbean governments. It is reasonable to presume that this helps to explain the fact that different post-colonial states have performed differently. As Banner himself acknowledges, there are 'considerable differences between Jamaica, with GDP per capita in 2019 of $5,500, and Barbados, with GDP per capita of $18,000 (which is an average for the world)'.[24] Indeed, not only has Barbados achieved the world average in GDP per capita, but in 2019 life expectancy at birth in post-slavery Barbados was 14 years higher than in post-slave-trading Nigeria,[25] literacy (in Barbados in 2014) was over 60 per cent higher (than in Nigeria in 2018),[26] and Gross National Income per capita in US$ in 2023 twelve times higher.[27]

IV

However, while post-colonial policy has been an important determinant of the fate of post-colonial economies in the Caribbean, Orlando Patterson makes a plausible argument that it has not been the only one. Colonial legacies have also played a role – in his view, a predominant one. A Professor of Sociology at Harvard University and former special advisor to Michael Manley, the democratic socialist Prime Minister of Jamaica from 1972–80, Patterson acknowledges that Jamaica's post-colonial failures 'began with the import-substitution/ modernization approach of the 1960s'.[28] (We should note that Peter Henry, a Jamaican-born economist at New York University, blames 'the failed democratic-socialist policies' of Manley's government in the 1970s.[29]) Nonetheless, Patterson argues, an explanation is needed for why economic policies that have failed in Jamaica have prospered in Barbados.[30] His answer is that the cause lies in their differing colonial inheritances, specifically the different political ethos that each country was bequeathed.[31]

It is important to take note, in passing, that Patterson recognises that colonial government and society took more than one form and produced more than one set of effects. He quotes with approval Atul Kohli's criticism of 'the tendency to homogenize the anti-developmental nature of all colonialism'.[32] This is, of course, a tendency well displayed by the likes of Beckles and Banner.

So, what was the relevant colonial legacy in Jamaica? The main element was the island's change of status in 1866, when it became a 'Crown colony', replacing its local, planter-dominated legislative assembly with direct rule from London. This was a response to the Morant Bay Rebellion of 1865 and its bloody and highly controversial suppression by Governor Eyre. The reform was welcomed by most coloured assembly-men, who represented the mixed-race middle class that had attained full civil liberties during slavery.[33]

On the one hand, the happy immediate result was the appointment of a governor 'of unusual competence and integrity', Sir John Peter Grant. During his 12-year appointment, Grant overhauled the education system, so that it provided elementary education for 'a substantially increased number of poor children (albeit still a small minority)', and he established island-wide medical facilities.[34] And during the subsequent 'classic period of stable colonial rule', which lasted until the 1930s, the leasing of Crown land led to 'the modest growth' of a relatively prosperous group of small farmers, who contributed substantially to the economy and were 'major economic innovators'.[35]

On the other hand, government by Crown officials accountable to London had the unhappy effect of removing

Jamaicans – except for 'a sprinkling' of local white and near-white coloureds – from positions of high responsibility in political, administrative and economic life: 'The mass of black Jamaicans faced complete institutional exclusion'. This was 'the major factor in the eventual postcolonial unpreparedness and mismanagement of the island', resulting in a political culture of clientelism associated with the drug trade and violence.[36]

The story in Barbados was very different. Whereas in Jamaica, land was available for subsistence farming and slaves could become independent peasants upon emancipation, in Barbados most cultivable land was already under sugar production, forcing freed slaves to continue working on the plantations.[37] This had the – eventually fortunate – effect of 'enculturating the Barbadian workforce to capitalist work norms'.[38] It enabled post-colonial Barbados to make the disciplined, free-market, neoliberal choices it did.[39]

A second important difference was that in Barbados, uniquely in the Caribbean, extremely poor whites comprised the bottom of the social heap, the class structure was economic rather than racial, and blacks were able to achieve a measure of upward social mobility through education.[40] Shortly after emancipation, pressed by the imperial authorities, planters in Barbados approved funds for elementary education, with the result that by 1844 there were 56 church-organised schools, mainly Anglican, and by mid-century black Barbadians were the most literate in the Caribbean. In the last three decades of the 1800s, educational opportunities were 'substantially increased' by the imperial authorities, so that fifty years later, in 1946, 91 per cent of the black population over the age of ten could read and write. The white rate was only seven points higher.[41]

Consequently, to a remarkable extent, Barbadians came to identify themselves with – and own – their British colonial inheritance. They became 'active agents in [the] imperial venture' of emancipating and civilising West Africa as missionaries and schoolteachers. As early as 1850 a black Barbadian became leader of an Anglican mission to what is now Gambia, followed five years later by another mission to Rio Pongas. Patterson endorses David Lowenthal's observation in the 1950s that Barbados was 'proud of . . . her unbroken connection with Britain'.[42] He also quotes Sir Courtney Blackman, a black Barbadian who became head of the nation's central bank, as saying in 2013 something 'unthinkable coming from a Jamaican': 'I found those white plantation men to be good men'.[43]

A third positive feature of independent Barbados's colonial inheritance was 'a colonial state with over three hundred years of continuous parliamentary rule by a local elite focused entirely on local issues and an efficient, highly educated bureaucracy, giving the nation extraordinary levels of state capacity'.[44]

The contemporary upshot of its colonial legacy is that, according to World Bank data on policy performance and institutional effectiveness, Barbados far outranks Jamaica and all the other states of Latin America and the Caribbean, and on two measures it even runs ahead of the major OECD countries (mainly Western Europe, North America, Japan and Australia).[45] Moreover, it is now 'a global model of parliamentary democracy'.[46]

Banner's argument for a basic continuity in equal misery from the era of slavery, via negligent imperial and colonial government, to present-day economic woes in the Caribbean does not begin to do justice to the facts. There was no uniform colonial legacy and there is no uniform post-colonial condition. Not every post-colonial state languishes economically: Barbados flourishes, thanks to its colonial inheritance. And even in Jamaica, which has languished, the record of imperial government was not entirely bad.

V

Nonetheless, it is asserted – not least, by the Brattle Report – that the living descendants of enslaved Africans in the Caribbean continue to suffer 'intergenerational trauma'.[47] The idea is that the original experience of enslavement suffered by their ancestors has impressed itself deeply on subsequent generations, notwithstanding formal emancipation, so that the psychological and social damage done in the 1700s and early 1800s still reverberates today. This commands at least superficial plausibility. Certainly, we know that the mental effects of grave, especially violent, physical or psychological injury can survive in an individual long after the injuring itself has ceased – say, in the form of lingering mistrust, fear, diffidence and resentment. This long-term psychic scarring is what is called 'trauma'. It is also equally plausible that the psychic scarring of an individual will affect their relationships, not least with their marital partner and their children. Their children will then themselves be scarred, affecting their relationships, marriages and children. And so forth.

This is, however, a universal phenomenon. There is nobody on earth whose ancestors did not suffer grievous injuries of several sorts. It follows that we are all affected, more or less, by historic injuries. But surely as time passes, and one generation succeeds another, the trace will tend to weaken, the scar become less inflamed, the effects attenuate. Moreover, other causes and choices – maybe beneficial and remedial – intervene. Even those who argue that contemporary African Americans suffer the effects of intergenerational trauma concede that they have also inherited legacies of healing and resilience.[48] As the anthropologist Didier Fassin and the psychiatrist Richard Rechtman have written, the concept of trauma is commonly used in such a way that it

> obscures the diversity and complexity of experiences. It conceals the way in which experiences take on multiple meanings in a collective history, in a personal life story . . . Having lived through an explosion . . . the destruction of one's home . . . the persecution of one's family . . . does not necessarily imply that one's experience is circumscribed by this event, or even that one desires that it be reduced to this event.[49]

What the distant past has bequeathed us may constrain and challenge us, but it is not our fate.

9

NAKED EMPEROR I: HILARY BECKLES

Sir Hilary Beckles, KA, is widely regarded as an authority on the history and effects of Caribbean slavery and is liberally and uncritically cited by advocates for reparations. However, his scholarship is not reliable.

I

Sir Hilary Beckles, KA, is much celebrated. Holding a PhD from the University of Hull and made Vice-Chancellor of the University of the West Indies, he has been showered with honours. He has been awarded honorary degrees by Hull, the Kwame Nkrumah University of Science and Technology, and the University of Glasgow. He has received the highest honour in the Order of Barbados, when he was made a Knight of St Andrew in 2007, and the highest honour among the Governor-General of Antigua and Barbuda's Faithful and Meritorious Awards, the Cross and Plaque, in 2021.

He is also the chairman of the CARICOM Reparations

Commission. This describes itself as 'a regional body created to establish the moral, ethical and legal case for the payment of Reparations by the Governments of all the former colonial powers and the relevant institutions of those countries, to the nations and people of the Caribbean Community for the Crimes against Humanity of Native Genocide, the Trans-Atlantic Slave Trade and a racialized system of chattel Slavery'.[1]

Beckles is liberally and uncritically invoked by advocates for reparations such as Maxine Berg, Pat Hudson and Michael Banner.[2] In *Britain's Slavery Debt: Reparations Now!*, for example, Banner prefaces the main text with a quotation of Beckles, which confidently asserts that, in respect of 'the multiple crimes against humanity they committed in the region', 'the evidentiary basis of the case [for reparations by Britain and other colonising nations] has long been established'.[3] It seems that Banner sought, and gained, Beckles's authoritative imprimatur, which appears as a commendation on his book's back cover.

However, judging by the hyperbolic rhetoric, the historical inaccuracy and the lack of intellectual rigour that characterises Beckles's 2013 work, *Britain's Black Debt: Reparations for Caribbean Slavery and Native Genocide*, his scholarship is generally not to be trusted.

II

Britain's Black Debt presents itself on its back cover as 'the first scholarly work that looks comprehensively at the reparations discussion in the Caribbean'.[4] Beckles's general view of British colonialism is expressed in his description of it as a 'criminal enrichment project'[5] and of its 'known features' as 'its terrorism of adults and ruthless exploitation of children; its maddening material poverty; and the racial brutality it bred within the prison known as the plantation'.[6] He claims that '[f]rom the West Indies, the British exported the financially successful model of African enslavement to the rest of the colonized world', and he refers to Queen Elizabeth II's apology in 1995 for 'the genocidal activities committed by the British' in New Zealand.[7]

This cartoonish reduction of 400 years of British colonial endeavour from North America, across Africa, to India and Australasia will seem wildly distorted to anyone who finds plausible the nuanced accounts given by Niall Ferguson in 2003, Bernard Porter in 2016, or me in 2023.[8] One immediate symptom of Beckles's politically charged inaccuracy is that the royal apology he refers to was for the punitive confiscation of Māori lands in 1865, which, however wrong, was a long, long way short of genocide.

Against the claim that Africans themselves were deeply

implicated in the slave trade, Beckles argues that they never reduced 'subordinate workers, political prisoners and others subject to criminal punishment' to the legal status of 'non-humans, perpetual property and reproductive chattels';[9] that this 'is the classic divide-and-rule defence in which victims are blamed for their victimization'; that '[t]he majority of African leaders over time opposed the slave trade' and '[f]or this they were destabilized and destroyed';[10] and that African chiefs were forced to raid for slaves under pain of attack and enslavement themselves.[11]

In response, I invite the reader to recall Chapter 5. In particular, I observe that the West African custom of burying 'servants' alive with their deceased master does rather imply a view of them as violently disposable property; that to blame African slave-traders is not to blame African slaves; that there are no historical grounds for the claim that African chiefs generally opposed the slave trade; and that, while it is possible that some chiefs felt themselves compelled by Europeans to raid for slaves, many of them were engaged in slave-raiding and trading for centuries before Europeans arrived on the scene.[12] The fact that, faced with the claim of African complicity, some West African states have withdrawn their support for the 'reparations movement' might be because of their recognition of the truth rather than because of Western intimidation, as Beckles speculates.[13]

III

On the issue of the extent to which Britain's wealth and power was built on the slave trade and slavery, Beckles is unequivocal: 'It is important for British society to acknowledge that its development as a nation-state, the transformation of its economy to sustainable industrialization, and its global standing as a super-power among nations were founded upon a crime against humanity in the form of racial chattel enslavement of African bodies and the global trafficking of these bodies for three hundred years'.[14] In adopting this view, he declares himself 'particularly indebted to Eric Williams, whose scholarship underpins much of this work'.[15] He is aware that Williams's thesis in *Capitalism and Slavery* has been criticised: 'Conservative ... economic historians launched a crusade against it. In most cases ... there were layers of ideology, distinctly Eurocentric and sometimes with racial undertones.'[16] Nevertheless, he argues that 'its continued capacity to stimulate further research speaks to its essential correctness'.[17]

In defence of his position he invokes Robin Blackburn, former editor of the *New Left Review* and author of *The Making of New World Slavery: From the Baroque to the Modern, 1492–1800*, and indirectly through him the Marxist tradition of British historiography, with its leading lights Eric Hobsbawm and Christopher Hill.[18] Such British scholars, steeped in the study of labour history and 'with a deep intellectual commitment to social justice', he tells us, have tended to treat the issues raised by Williams 'more fairly'. Knowing the tendency for capital to subject labour to a basic subsistence level, they have recognised the importance of African enslavement to the rise of industrial capitalism in general.[19]

In addition to Marxist historians, Beckles also press-gangs some critics of Williams. The 'ardent critic' David Richardson, he argues, nonetheless 'essentially agreed with the fundamental correctness of Williams's research' when he wrote (in 1987) that

> Caribbean-based demands may have accounted for 12 per cent of the growth of English industrial output in the quarter century before 1776 ... Although West Indian and related trades provided a more modest stimulus to the growth of British industrial production than Williams imagined, they nevertheless played a more prominent part in fostering industrial changes and export growth in Britain during the third quarter of the eighteenth century than most historians have assumed.[20]

And summarising Kenneth Morgan's position, Beckles writes that '[f]or Morgan, the slavery system was not the cause of British development. It was a "stimulus". Williams would not have disagreed.'[21]

Beckles's case here is riddled with flaws. First, he does not engage at all with the 'conservative' economic historians who disagreed with Williams. Indeed, he does not even name them. Instead, he summarily dismisses their views as distorted by political 'ideology' (unlike his own) and by racism.

Second, the works of recognised experts on transatlantic slavery such as David Eltis, Seymour Drescher and David Brion Davis appear in his bibliography, but receive no mention at all in the text. (It was Davis who declared of Williams's thesis in 2010 that it 'has now been wholly discredited by other scholars'.[22])

Third, he identifies himself with a Marxist-Leninist reading of colonial economics, which has generally not fared well when its theory has been made accountable to the empirical data.[23] As mentioned in the previous chapter, the neo-Marxist dogma that colonialism was simply a bloodsucker, greedily extracting wealth from colonies and hoarding it in the imperial fatherland, does not survive contact with the empirical work of Rudolf von Albertini.[24]

Fourth, Beckles's claim that Richardson and Morgan end up confirming Williams's thesis is just not true. That thesis was not that the profits from the slave trade were merely an economic stimulus – no one denies that – but that they made 'an *enormous* contribution to Britain's industrial development' (the emphasis is mine).[25] That is Beckles's position, too: Britain's wealth and power were '*founded* upon a crime against humanity' (the emphasis, again, is mine). In contrast, Richardson judges the contribution of the slave trade and slavery to be 'more modest' – 12 per cent is significant, but hardly enormous.[26] And Morgan reckons that it would be 'incorrect' to claim that the profits from the trade were 'a major stimulus for industrialization in Britain', but rather that they played 'a significant, though not decisive part' in its evolution.[27]

Fifth and finally, Beckles (like Berg, Hudson and Banner) is completely oblivious to the century and a half of costly British imperial endeavour in suppressing the slave trade and the institution of slavery worldwide – from Brazil, across Africa, to India and Australasia. For a fuller account, I refer the reader to Chapter 7.

For all these reasons, I conclude that Hilary Beckles's work is not generally trustworthy and should not be taken at face value as authoritative. On close inspection, this celebrated emperor proves to be considerably naked.

10

NAKED EMPEROR II: THE BRATTLE REPORT

The 2023 Brattle Report presents itself as an academically authoritative calculation of what monetary sums are owed by whom as reparations for historic slavery. It is nothing of the sort. Rather, it is the product of a group of activists, some with PhDs, who have avoided exposing their prejudices to critical testing. The result is a document that displays historical ignorance, ignores awkward data, presents the controversial as incontrovertible, and satisfies itself with threadbare reasoning. A second naked emperor struts across the stage.

I

'[T]he total harm estimated from enslavement is between us$100 trillion and us$131 trillion', concludes *The Report on Reparations for Transatlantic Chattel Slavery in the Americas and the Caribbean.*[1] Britain's share comes in at over us$26 trillion (£20 trillion), which is fifteen times the annual budget of the UK government in March 2025.

The report was published in June 2023 and comprises two documents. The first is an introduction by Patrick Robinson, a Jamaican jurist;[2] the second, a *Quantification of Reparations for Transatlantic Chattel Slavery*, prepared for the University of the West Indies and the American Society of International Law's (ASIL) Second Symposium on Reparations under International Law by the Brattle Group, a Boston-based consulting firm.[3] Together, they are commonly referred to as 'the Brattle Report' and I shall treat them as a single entity.

The Brattle Report wears the appearance of legal and academic authority. Patrick Robinson is a former President of the International Criminal Tribunal for the former Yugoslavia and a member of the International Court of Justice, and he is the recipient of the Order of Jamaica for services to international law. Robinson convened an Advisory Committee, which, with sponsorship from the University of the West Indies and ASIL, organised two symposia on reparations in 2021 and 2023, of which the Brattle Report is the fruit. Among the academics engaged by the committee was David Eltis, Robert M. Woodruff Professor Emeritus of History at Emory University and eminent historian of transatlantic slavery. In his introduction, Robinson says of Eltis that he produced a database of the number of enslaved Africans transported, without which the Brattle Report would not have been possible, and that 'he was kind enough to meet with the Advisory

Committee'.[4] However, appearances deceive. The intellectual quality of the report is poor, sometimes risibly so. And David Eltis's contribution was limited to a database already publicly available, together with participation in a single telephonic 'group chat'.[5]

II

The main body of the Brattle Report consists of an attempt to quantify what monetary reparations are owed by whom. This assumes a justification for reparations, which is mainly presented in Robinson's introduction but also appears in the *Quantification*. In the light of what has been argued in this book so far, that justification suffers from three basic flaws. First, it makes no mention at all of African complicity in European slave-trading. Second, it makes no mention at all of the British Empire's sustained and expensive commitment to suppressing slavery worldwide from 1807. And third, it asserts, invoking Hilary Beckles, that 'transatlantic chattel slavery as an atrocity exemplifying man's inhumanity to man has never been surpassed'.[6]

On the legality of European and American slavery, Robinson reports that the first International Symposium on the Lawfulness of Transatlantic Chattel Slavery concluded that it was 'unlawful on the basis of the law applicable at that time'. The applicable law comprised two kinds: first, that of African countries; and second, the normative principle of humanity, recognised in the 1814 Treaty of Ghent between Britain and the USA, and in the 1815 Vienna Declaration adopted by Britain, France, Spain and Portugal.[7]

However, if it is really true that all African 'countries' in the seventeenth and eighteenth centuries outlawed slavery, then there was widespread African breaking of African international law – for which Africans were responsible. And unless they recognised what reigned as law between African peoples, Europeans were not bound by it. What is more, neither Robinson nor any of his colleagues seem to have noticed that the Treaty of Ghent and the Vienna Declaration occurred only *after* – and *because* – Britain had abolished the slave trade, was trying to persuade other nations to follow suit, and was anticipating the demise of slavery itself. In other words, the international establishment of the 'normative principle of humanity' was an important step in the British Empire's efforts to make slavery illegal worldwide.

III

Of course, for reparations to make sense, a plausible case needs to be made for strong causal connections between historic slavery and the present woes of the descendants of slaves. Here, the Brattle Report is strong on assertions and weak on substantiation. It tells us confidently that 'the damage caused by TCS [transatlantic chattel slavery] is ... deeply entrenched and pervasive'.[8] It argues for a causal connection – but mainly between wrongful acts perpetrated by slavery and injuries suffered by the original victims, not between historic wrongdoing and the victims' descendants.[9]

When it does turn to the crucial and highly controversial issue of the effects of slavery after emancipation in 1833, it manages to give its attention for just over two pages and focuses mostly on racist discrimination: 'the essential feature of the continuing harm is discriminatory treatment'.[10] It cites the Barbados Slave Code of 1661 and Jamaica's Morant Bay Rebellion of 1865, as if the effects on all the West Indian colonies were uniform. And it holds 'TCS and colonialism' directly responsible for 'the structural and systemic forms of modern-day racism', ignoring the disruptive fact that Britain's abolition movement of the late 1700s and its anti-slavery policies from 1807 were premised on the egalitarian conviction that all persons are basically equal under God, regardless of race and cultural development. It also takes for granted that 'modern-day racism' in the US and the UK, for example, is identical.[11] Then, on this thin, patchy and dubious basis, it puffs itself up into a gravely judicious posture, grandly concluding that 'on the basis of proof on a balance of probabilities there is a sufficiently direct and certain causal nexus' between historic slavery and the descendants of slaves.[12]

IV

On quantifying reparations owed in monetary terms, the Brattle Group's team is frank: it is 'a daunting task'. It wisely admits that much harm cannot be quantified, including the deprivation of citizenship and identity. However, it also admits, startlingly, that even the 'essential feature' of continuing harm, racism, is among the unquantifiable elements.[13]

For the post-enslavement period, the report offers 'a summary measure based on wealth differentials between people of African descent in the Americas and the Caribbean and the descendants of the enslavers'. So, subtracting the present lower wealth of formerly colonised countries from the present higher wealth of former colonisers gives us a wealth differential that is a monetary measure of the harm that deserves reparation. This method, it reassures us, is 'established in the academic literature on reparations'.[14]

That may be so, but an appeal to academic authority does not render a prima facie crazy idea any more sensible. It is indubitable that the present condition of former slave colonies owes something to their having been colonised. But, as we saw above in Chapter 8, that includes good things as well as bad. Further, the present condition of former colonies also owes a lot to the policies of post-colonial governments in the past sixty years, as even Orlando Patterson admits. Further still, the superior wealth of former colonial countries, while owing something modest to profits from slavery, owes much more to other factors – in Britain's case, to industrial, financial and institutional creativity. It follows that the gap in present wealth cannot sensibly be read as a monetary measure of harm caused and reparations owed.

V

The appearance of intellectual gravitas and objectivity in which the Brattle Report strives to wrap itself is a mirage. Its historical ignorance and omissions, its presentation of controversial issues as incontrovertible, and its shoddy reasoning all indicate that those involved did not care to expose their common prejudices to critical testing outside their activist circle. Consequently, this would-be emperor, too, is naked.

11

MAKING AMENDS FOR HISTORIC WRONGS

The making of amends to the wronged by those culpable of wrongdoing is moral common sense. But making historic reparations to the descendants of those enslaved two centuries ago by members of a society most of whose ancestors had nothing to do with slavery is not so obviously sensible. The riotous jungle of history obscures the causal pathways.

I

It is moral common sense that where someone has wronged another, he should repent, apologise, and either supply the loss or repair the damage. Only thus can reconciliation happen. So far, so straightforward. However, what makes good sense in interpersonal relations does not always make such good sense at a political level.

For example, in 1997 British Prime Minister Tony Blair made a public apology to the Irish people for the Great

Famine that had befallen Ireland 150 years before. His gesture was very well received by many of those at whom it was
directed. Yet, Mr Blair himself was not responsible for the
famine and no one alive in Ireland had suffered it. Moreover,
the extent to which the British government of the time
deserved blame for what happened is, to this day, a highly
controversial issue.[1] So, strictly speaking, Tony Blair did not
repent or apologise, and the Irish people did not forgive him.
And yet a measure of reconciliation was achieved.

What happened in 1997 was not exactly an apology, but
it was analogous to it. The context was the Peace Process in
Northern Ireland, designed to bring an end to three decades
of intermittent bloodshed that had killed over 3500 people in
the province. That process involved not just the UK government and Northern Irish politicians and paramilitary leaders,
but also the government of the Republic of Ireland, whose
consent was essential. Blair was aware that the antagonism
towards the British of many Irish people found its focus in
the Great Famine of the 1840s, for which, rightly or wrongly,
they blamed the British. So, for perfectly well-intentioned
political reasons, the Prime Minister decided to make the
public gesture of an 'apology'. In so doing, he was not assuming personal responsibility, nor was he necessarily agreeing
with Irish nationalists that the British government of the day
was blameworthy. Strictly speaking, what he was saying was

something like this: 'We British acknowledge and sympathise with the resentment that you Irish feel. With you, we lament the terrible suffering that befell Ireland 150 years ago. And we want to assure you that, were such a thing to happen again today, we would do everything possible to stop it.'

Apology and repentance find their natural place in the intimate relationship between individual persons. On the political stage, they become analogous – weaker versions of their proper selves.

II

For sure, some political analogies are stronger than others. A stronger one than Tony Blair's 'apology' was the German government's 'repentance' of the Nazi regime's theft of Jewish property, in the form of restitution or compensation, after the Second World War. In that case, the identities of the Jewish wronged and the Nazi wrongdoers, and the close relationship between original victims and surviving family members, were all clear enough. And the harm done was definite and quantifiable. In these circumstances, reparation and compensation made good sense.

The passage of time, however, muddies the waters. As the moral philosopher Onora O'Neill has written:

claims to compensation have to show that continuing loss or harm resulted from past injury. This is all too often impossible where harms have been caused by ancient or distant wrongs . . . Is everybody who descends (in part) from those who were once enslaved or colonised still being harmed by those now ancient and distant misdeeds? Can we offer a clear enough account of the causation of current harms to tell where compensation is owed? Can we show who ought to do the compensating?[2]

The riotous jungle of history overgrows and obscures the causal pathways.

In the case of historic British slavery, the victims themselves are, of course, all long dead and – short of God, an afterlife and a Final Judgement – they lie forever beyond the reach of restitution or compensation. As for their twenty-first-century descendants, their present condition, while perhaps owing something to the enslavement of their ancestors, also owes much to events and choices in the almost 200 years since emancipation. Can we be sure that they would have been better off had their ancestors remained in West Africa – some as slaves and sacrificial funeral fodder? Are there not some descendants of slaves who now prosper rather more than some descendants of slave-owners? And have not some of the latter devoted their tainted inheritance to charitable purposes, perhaps even anti-slavery endeavours?[3]

Further, if reparations are demanded of nation-states that presided over historic slave-trading and slavery – such as Britain – surely the tax-paying citizenry of those nations includes a majority of people whose ancestors had nothing whatsoever to do with enslaving others. Indeed, it even includes the descendants of slaves. How, then, can it be fair to expect them to shoulder the burden of funding reparations?

Besides, if the intention is to right grave historic wrongs, why should *slavery* be the sole focus? The plight of medieval serfs or early industrial workers dwelling in urban slums may have been better than that of slaves toiling in the West Indies, but not very much better. Nor was that of white indentured servants who also toiled in the plantations. As Richard Vernon puts it, the list of all those who suffered at the hands of 'the states of the eighteenth, nineteenth and twentieth centuries, whose failures of responsibility were almost universally appalling', is long and includes women, children, industrial workers, religious minorities, soldiers and sailors.[4] Out of all the eligible candidates, how can we justify selecting black slaves?

Moreover, why should *British* slavery be the focus? If the historic injustice of slavery is to be rectified, then it needs to be done fairly and across the board. If the British are to be presented with a bill for compensation, then so should the descendants of the inland African chiefs who sold other Africans to the slave-traders, as well as the descendants of the Arab slave-traders who sold the slaves to the Europeans on the coast.[5] They all profited too. And the British themselves should seek compensation from the descendants of the Barbary corsairs, who raided Cornwall in the 1600s and carted off whole villages into slavery on the Mediterranean coast of North Africa. If the British, then also the Americans, since, in its early years, the United States spent a fifth of its entire national budget in tribute to the pirate states of Algiers and Tripoli, in order to stop their raids on its ships and enslavement of their crews. Yesterday's oppressors were often the day before yesterday's victims. In a letter published in *The Times* some years ago, a former British diplomat recounted a conversation he had had shortly after Nigeria's independence with one of the country's new rulers. The ruler was pressing the case for Britain to compensate the Nigerians for decades of colonial oppression. After listening intently, the diplomat's turn to reply came. 'I entirely agree', he said. 'And you shall have your compensation – just as soon as we get ours from the Romans.'[6]

In the face of these intractable complications, the legal philosopher Jeremy Waldron concludes that our focus should be on addressing present injustices rather than trying to untangle historic injustices: 'it is the impulse to justice now that should lead the way . . . not the reparation of something whose wrongness is understood primarily in relation to conditions that no longer obtain. Entitlements . . . fade with time, counterfactuals . . . are impossible to verify, injustices . . . are overtaken by circumstances.'[7] O'Neill agrees with him:

> Compensation is required for present harm caused by past wrongdoing, not simply for current disadvantage *however caused.* Unless we can trace the causal pathways, we cannot tell who has gained from ancestral wrongdoing and should now shoulder the costs of compensating those whose present disadvantage was caused by past wrongdoing. It may therefore make more sense . . . to argue for a distributive – or redistributive – account of aspects of justice, which seeks action to redress present disadvantage, *whatever its origins.*[8]

This was the response given by Canada's Prime Minister, Pierre Trudeau, when he was pressed to redress historic injustice. Quoting President John F. Kennedy in 1972, he said: 'We will be just in our time. This is all we can do. We must be just today.'[9]

12

THE CHURCH OF ENGLAND'S RUSH
TO REPENTANCE

*In 2023 the Church Commissioners of England committed
the Church of England to begin to make reparations for its
involvement in transatlantic slavery. Yet, as a rationale,
they offered only unargued assumptions, most of which are
untrue. The policy runs out way ahead of evidence and
reason and implies a shocking lack of due diligence.*

I

In November 2023 the Church Commissioners of England,
the body responsible for administering the property assets
of the Church of England, committed the Church to deploy
an initial £100 million of those assets over nine years to
establish an investment fund, which, with the help of others,
they aim to grow to £1 billion.[1] The funds are to be used to
support a programme of 'impact investment, research and
engagement', aimed at improving the opportunities open to
communities 'affected by historic slavery'. In addition, the

Commissioners intend to fund further research into, and education programmes about, the Church's historic 'links' to slavery. These commitments were made in response to the discovery that the Queen Anne's Bounty, an eighteenth-century forerunner of the Church Commissioners' endowment devoted to supplementing the income of poorer clergy, had 'links' with African chattel enslavement. It aims to 'address some of the past wrongs'.[2]

Explanations are given in two documents. The first, the *Church Commissioners' Research into Historic Links with Transatlantic Chattel Slavery*, says this:

> In 2019, the Church Commissioners through reflection became more conscious of the fact that the transatlantic slave economy played a significant role in shaping the economy, society and Church we have today. The trade in enslaved African people was responsible for inflicting much pain and misery on people of African descent in particular but also on other groups around the world who have experienced deep injustices. It contributed to both the racial and class divisions and tensions we experience today in our society and, regrettably, in our Church ... The decision to embark upon this journey of understanding was timely. Less than a year later, George Floyd was murdered and churches, institutions

and corporations throughout the country and wider society developed a heightened interest in developing an understanding of our past in order to create a more just future for us all.[3]

The second document, *Oversight Group Recommendations to the Board of Governors: Healing, Repair, and Justice*, is less restrained: 'The immense wealth accrued by the Church Commissioners has always been interwoven with the history of African chattel enslavement', it tells us. 'African chattel enslavement was central to the growth of the British economy of the 18th and 19th centuries and the nation's wealth thereafter.'[4] Now, the Commissioners acknowledge a

strand of complicity in an abominable trade that still scars the lives of billions . . . the cruelty of a multinational white establishment that deprived tens of millions of Africans of life and liberty . . . has continuing toxic consequences resulting from the denial of equal access to healthcare, education, employment, justice, and capital . . . Crimes against humanity rooted in African chattel enslavement have caused damage so vast it will require patient effort spanning generations to address. But we can start today . . .[5]

And we start, by beginning to make reparations: 'At the heart of reparations is the idea of repair: repair of damage caused by past injustice which continues via present injustice'.[6] The £100 million is the Church's initial reparative response to the 'historic pool of capital tainted by its involvement in African chattel enslavement: Queen Anne's Bounty'.[7]

We find the same rationale in allied documents. In one, entitled 'The Church Commissioners for England: Historic Links to African Chattel Enslavement. Frequently Asked Questions', the commitment of £100 million is presented as a first, reparatory step in addressing the Church's 'shameful past' by trying to undo '[t]he legacy of this evil [that] impacts the lives of many people'.[8] But beyond repentance another motive is admitted, too: 'We believe that by addressing our past transparently ... the Church and its teachings will be more relevant to more people ... Visibly demonstrating that the Church of England is for all will help to make it more relevant to more people across our nation ...'.[9]

II

Observe how the rationale given for making reparations depends on a set of assertions: that the Church's 'immense wealth ... has always been interwoven' with enslavement; that slavery was 'central' to Britain's economic growth and prosperity; that slavery was perpetrated by a 'white establishment' upon Africans; and that today's descendants of slaves two centuries ago continue to suffer the effects of ancestral enslavement.

Every one of these claims, however, is dubious. As already discussed in these pages, the contribution of slave-trading and slavery to Britain's economic development is a highly controversial matter, but most economic historians reckon it was somewhere between marginal and modest.[10] Slavery was perpetrated on black Africans by other black Africans long before it was perpetrated by a 'white establishment'. And between abolition in 1834 and the present day, all sorts of other causes have intervened to complicate, dilute and even reverse the effects of slavery.

As for the Queen Anne's Bounty, it was barely involved in slave-trading at all.[11] The story is this. The South Sea Company was established in 1711 'to absorb short-term unfunded government debt by converting it into company shares that could be traded on the stock market. In return, the government paid interest to the South Sea Company which then went to investors.'[12] Two years later, in 1713, when war with Spain ended in the Treaty of Utrecht, the Company acquired the privileges of trading a certain number of slaves into Spanish colonies, as well as importing a ship's worth of merchandise per annum. The main attraction was the lucrative latter. Still, the acquisition was controversial, with almost 30 per cent of shareholders voting against it as likely to be unprofitable.[13] From that point on, shareholders could profit in two ways: through a government annuity paid on the shares and through commerce with Spanish colonies. The latter comprised only a very small part of its financial operations. It was also very uncertain, being frequently interrupted by war in 1718–20, 1727–9 and 1739, after which it ceased entirely. And it did prove unprofitable.

In 1720 the Queen Anne's Bounty converted a portion of its holdings of short-term government securities into South Sea Company shares, resulting, as it happened, in a serious loss. In 1723, since many shareholders wanted to avoid participating in the Company's trade altogether, the existing shares were formally divided into 'annuities' and trading stock ('shares'). Preferring to invest in the former alone, the Bounty chose to sell most of the latter five years later and all of them by 1730. Richard Dale, Professor Emeritus of International Banking at the University of Southampton and author of the 2004 book, *The First Crash: Lessons from the South Sea Bubble*,[14] has commented:

If the Bounty managers had wished to benefit from the slaving business, they would have invested in the Company's shares; but, with one minor exception in 1720 – when the slave trade was shut down owing to war with Spain – they chose to avoid the risks and rewards of the commercial business and invested, instead, in what were essentially government-backed debt instruments.[15]

He continues:

The [Church] Commissioners conclude that '. . . a significant portion of the Bounty's income during the 18th century was derived from sources that may be linked to transatlantic slavery, principally interest and dividends on South Sea Company annuities'.[16] This conclusion is misleading on several fronts. First, no investor in the South Sea Company benefited financially from the slave trade, since it was consistently loss-making. Second, the Church Bounty did not even stand to benefit from the trade, because it declined to buy shares in the Company. Third, the investments that it did make, in South Sea annuities, represented, at one remove, claims on the Government which had no connection with the trade in slaves. Finally, it is grossly misleading to suggest, as the church report does, that all South Sea investors were consciously investing in slave-trading voyages.[17]

However, it is true that the managers of the Queen Anne's Bounty did hold on to trading stock after trade resumed in

June 1721, selling nearly all of them by 1729 and all by 1730. Lawrence Goldman and Robert Tombs comment:

> However, while the connection of the Bounty with the slave trade was reprehensible and a proper cause of regret, it was certainly not the source of 'a historic pool of capital'. The South Sea Company never made any profit from slave trading, and the Bounty did not derive any income from slave trading during the brief period when it held shares in the Company. On the contrary, its 1720 investment in shares made a disastrous loss, equal to 14 percent of its total portfolio.[18]

François Velde, senior research economist at the Federal Reserve Bank of Chicago, is unequivocal in concurring:

> Did any of that money [the Bounty's revenue from the Company] come from the slave trade? No, simply because the South Sea Company never made any profits from the slave trade. Although we don't have the Company's books, we have a summary of the Company's income and expenditure flows from 1720 to 1732 (Report of the Committee appointed to inspect and examine the Several Accompts of the South-Sea Company 1733, 24–30) which show that the trade account had a negative balance.[19]

III

In addition to revenue from the South Sea Company, the Queen Anne's Bounty also comprised benefactions. According to the *Church Commissioners' Research into Historic Links*, these generated around 14 per cent of the Bounty's income in the eighteenth century.[20] Its analysis of benefaction registers between 1713 and 1850 has led it to conclude that 'the proportion of benefactions derived from individuals who were considered to have a very high (8%) or high (22%) likelihood of potentially being linked to the transatlantic trade in enslaved people was overall about 30% of all benefactions that were received by Queen Anne's Bounty'.[21]

Note, however, the highly speculative basis of the claim. The factors allowed to determine likelihood included simply 'being active at the time of the South Sea Bubble; involvement in politics (including being a member of the House of Lords); being linked to cities that were heavily involved in transatlantic slavery such as Bristol, Liverpool, London and Manchester; being linked to industries that relied on transatlantic slavery such as cotton, copper or iron; and having naval connections'.[22] Of course, it would have been perfectly possible to have had every one of these associations and yet to have had no involvement in slave-trading at all.

In one section the document explains that its calculations

include benefactions that 'appeared' to have been made by relatives or descendants of Edward Colston. A Bristol merchant, Colston was, for twelve years from 1680 to 1692, a member of the Royal African Company, which traded in slaves from West Africa. In some cases, it is clear that the benefactions 'were derived directly' from Colston. But not all: 'it is possible', for example, 'that the monies provided by Alexander Colston were his own and were not derived from the transatlantic trade in enslaved people'.[23] However, even where benefactions did derive directly from Colston, it is impossible to know how far they included proceeds from slave-trading – or whether they did at all. After all, Colston lived for 84 years and was engaged from the age of 18 in a wide range of commercial activity:

He conducted an extensive wine and oil trade with Spain and Portugal, becoming probably the largest importer of Levantine fruits at Bristol; he also imported sugar from the New World . . . From 1672 to 1674 he sent small shipments of goods from London to Tangier, Lisbon, the Canary Islands, Cadiz and Rotterdam, exporting textiles such as double bays, perpets and serges, and importing wine . . . In 1686, he was still exporting textiles and importing wine and had begun trading with various Mediterranean ports. By that time he had become a regular trader in Newfoundland cod to Naples.[24]

What is more, even the Royal African Company's trade with West Africa was not confined to slaves, but also included gold, silver and ivory. As Kenneth Morgan observes, Colston's 'European commodities trading, financial investments, and lending activities also . . . contributed to his great wealth'.[25]

In the end, then, what do we know about the involvement of the Bounty in slave-trading? We know that it bought South Sea Company shares during a period when, thanks to war, the Company was not involved in trade with Spanish colonies at all. We know that it retained some trading stock from the end of the war in June 1721 and 1730. We know that it made no money out of it. We know that it chose to divest itself of that stock over those nine years. And we know that some benefactions might have derived from profits made from slave-trading. However, we do not know whether benefactions loosely 'linked' to slave-trading actually derived from it. Nor do we know whether benefactions from merchants who were certainly engaged in slave-trading were based on profits made *there* as distinct from the many other commercial ventures they were engaged in.

Notwithstanding this, the Church Commissioners have put their signatures to documents that assert that 'the transatlantic slave economy played a significant role in shaping the . . . Church we have today' and that '[t]he immense wealth accrued by the Church Commissioners has always been interwoven with the history of African chattel enslavement'.[26] Both these statements run out boldly ahead of the meagre evidence. Why? The answer lies in another statement, namely, that the Commissioners' assets include a 'historic pool of capital tainted by its involvement in African chattel enslavement'.[27] The thinking seems to be that *any* historic part of the assets that comprised profits from slave-trading has infected the contemporary whole, which is 'interwoven' with it.[28] What should we think of this? On the one hand, the Commissioners' assets – just like any inheritance built up over centuries – will have been accumulated in ways that involve elements of wrongdoing, be it fraud, theft or exploitation. Since all accumulation is achieved by sinners, there is no such thing as a pure inheritance. On the other hand, as argued above in Chapter II, it does not necessarily follow that we must deploy our inheritance to unravel history and reverse the centuries-old wrongdoing that helped to produce it. We did not do the wrong. Those wronged are all dead. And between then and now, much else may have intervened to enable their descendants to transcend the effects.

IV

We have observed how several important things that the Church Commissioners do say are not true. Now, we need to observe an important thing that they do not say. They make no mention at all of Anglican involvement in the dogged, half-century-long campaign to abolish the slave trade and slavery; or of the fact that the British were among the first peoples in the history of the world to abolish them; or of Anglican involvement in the subsequent century and a half of British imperial endeavour to suppress slavery worldwide from Brazil to New Zealand.

It is particularly egregious that the Church Commissioners should have failed to take into account all those Christian missionaries who, following David Livingstone, risked – and sometimes spent – their lives endeavouring to end the slave trade in Africa. Among them was the Anglican bishop John Mackenzie, who died horribly of blackwater fever in what is now Mozambique in 1862 at the age of 37.

In a sermon preached in Christ Church Cathedral, Zanzibar, on 12 May 2024, the then Archbishop of Canterbury, Justin Welby, while acknowledging the missionaries' fight against slavery, went on to criticise them for treating Africans as inferior and to confess that 'we must repent and look at what we did in Zanzibar'.[29] This is odd, since what the British did in Zanzibar during the second half of the nineteenth century was to force the Sultan to end the slave trade. As for racial prejudice among missionaries, Alexander Chula, who taught in Malawi for three years and recounts his experience in *Goodbye, Dr Banda*, writes this:

I am curious to know who exactly the former Archbishop had in mind. Mackenzie's successors gave everything they had to the region, and their graves litter Malawi, still venerated today. They committed to sharing the lives of local peoples and ... approached their cultures with a curiosity and respect seldom matched by Western visitors today. The imputation that they treated Africans as inferior dishonours men who died precisely because they considered Africans as worthy of that sacrifice as anyone.[30]

Certainly, it dishonours David Livingstone, who wrote as follows in 1871:

I have no prejudice against [the Africans'] colour; indeed, anyone who lives long among them forgets that they are black and feels that they are just fellow men ... If a comparison were instituted, and Manyuema, taken at random, placed opposite say members of the Anthropological Society of London, clad like them in kilts of grass cloth, I should like to take my place among the Manyuema, on the principle of preferring the company of my betters.[31]

V

Finally, we should observe how, apart from the forensic analysis of the Queen Anne's Bounty, none of the Church Commissioners' assertions is supported by an argument, presenting evidence and negotiating controversies. Argument, however, is surely needed. The moral duty to repent of wrongs we have done and to repair them as far as possible is Christian common sense. And while we cannot exactly repent of wrongs other people have done, if we have benefited from their wrongdoing, we do have a responsibility to try to correct it.[32] So far, so straightforward. Things become more complicated, however, the more time elapses between the past wrong and the present. The onerous effects of the original wrong become mixed up with – and maybe ameliorated by – other effects, so that the descendants of victims do not suffer as the victims themselves did. And historic beneficiaries of the wrong may already have invested time, money and lives in trying to correct it.

Moreover, as I have argued, history is replete with wrongs from which we now benefit. Little or nothing that we inherit is without historic taint. The present Church of England occupies cathedrals and churches seized by the state from Rome during the Reformation. Some of its present wealth was almost certainly squeezed out of overworked and under-rewarded medieval serfs and nineteenth-century industrial workers.

So, the question of which past wrongs to address and how best to address them is a complicated one that needs a careful answer. Yet, nowhere have the Church Commissioners felt it necessary to give one. Indeed, they surrendered the matter entirely to members of an 'Oversight Group' whose subsequent recommendations they rubber-stamped. But this 'Oversight Group', while sporting 'a great diversity of skills and backgrounds',[33] contained no significant intellectual diversity at all. Evidently, they all shared the same basic assumptions, which they saw no need to subject to critical testing. The failure of due diligence – on the part of Church Commissioners, no less – is shocking.[34]

13

IN SUM: WHY SLAVERY REPARATIONS DON'T ADD UP

In the light of everything that has been said in the foregoing chapters, let me sum up the case against the making of reparations for historic slavery by the British.

First, good, humble moral judgement pays close attention to circumstances. So, when judging British involvement in slave-trading and slavery over two centuries ago, attention should be paid to their contexts, the first of which was the universality of both the trade and the institution.

Second, the humiliation and cruelty of British slave-trading and slavery over a century and a half was unique neither in kind nor degree. Many, many other peoples did similarly lamentable things, not least Africans and Arabs, and for a much longer period of time. The racially discriminatory fingering of the British is unfair and politically opportunistic.

Third, if, as most economic historians think, Britain's industrial prosperity owed something small or modest to slave-trading and slavery, it owed a lot more to a wide range of other factors.

Fourth, the involvement of the Church of England's Queen Anne's Bounty in slave-trading was indirect, brief and unprofitable.

Fifth, the British were among the first peoples in the history of the world to abolish both slave-trading and slavery itself, not least thanks to sustained agitation by Christians, many of them Anglican, some of them black.

Sixth, the British went on to do penance for slavery by spending resources of money, ships and lives in using imperial power to suppress slavery worldwide for a century and a half. Among them were Anglican lobbyists in London, naval officers and ratings at sea, and missionaries abroad.

Seventh, the British government's decision to pay compensation to slave-owners for their loss of property upon emancipation was made in part as a necessary political compromise to enable the passing of emancipatory legislation, and in part to prevent the economic collapse of plantations, upon which many free blacks would continue to depend for wage-earning employment.

Eighth, it is not true that British emancipation made no beneficial difference at all to the lives of any of the former slaves. Nor is it true that British colonial government did nothing to facilitate economic development and education in the West Indies.

Ninth, the current economic woes of some Caribbean

states owe much, at least, to post-colonial mismanagement.

And tenth, Britain today is not systemically racist. Indeed, it is one of the least racist countries on earth. And such racism as does persist today cannot be traced back to historic slavery through 'colonialism', since for the second half of its life the British Empire was committed to anti-slavery on the basis of fundamental racial equality.

The case for the British making reparations for slavery does not add up. That is not to say, however, that they should not give aid to Caribbean states. Britain is a relatively prosperous country, partly thanks to its own endeavours, but also thanks to good fortune. It is right that those with more should give to those with less, if the latter need help and the former can afford to give it – all other things being equal. So, in principle, Britain should aid other less well-off countries. However, wealthy though Britain may be, it does not have the resources to save the whole world. Therefore, it must select which parts to help. And one reasonable criterion for selection is historical association. So, for example, since Britain did have responsibility for the welfare of West Indian colonies for several centuries, and since it retains cultural, institutional, legal and sometimes constitutional links with post-colonial Caribbean states, it would make sense to target its aid there rather than elsewhere.

14

CONCLUSION: SO WHY THE LUST FOR SELF-CONDEMNATION?

I

As we have just seen, in Britain the Church Commissioners have committed an initial £100 million of funds to serve as slavery reparations, on grounds that turn out to be historically, empirically and morally spurious. And all with an astonishing lack of due diligence. Yet, this unseemly rush to irrational repentance is but one symptom of a larger malaise infecting English-speaking countries that are former members of the British Empire.

II

In Australia, there is the extraordinary career of Bruce Pascoe's *Dark Emu*. Published in 2014, this book argues that Aborigines, far from being primitive nomads, developed the first egalitarian society, invented democratic government, eschewed 'imperial warfare', pioneered complex fishing technology and were sophisticated agriculturalists. Such was the morally superior civilisation that white colonisers trashed in their greed, racist contempt and relentless violence.[1] *Dark Emu* was named Book of the Year and received the Indigenous Writers' Prize in the 2016 New South Wales Premier's Literary Awards. It has sold more than 360,000 copies and has been made the subject of an ABC documentary.

And yet, while enthusiastically praised for challenging conventional views about Aboriginal culture and popularising the topic, it has been widely and plausibly criticised for being factually inaccurate. Although not a professional academic, Peter O'Brien has forensically dismantled it in *Bitter Harvest*, systematically exposing the many gaps between claim and evidence.[2] And in *Farmers or Hunter Gatherers: The Dark Emu Debate* (2021), eminent anthropologist Peter Sutton and archaeologist Keryn Walshe, while vigorously rejecting the description of Aboriginal culture as 'primitive', nevertheless dismiss Pascoe's claims for Aboriginal agriculture and aquaculture and expose his editing of primary sources to make them appear to support his thesis.[3] Reviewers have described their book variously as 'formidably well researched', 'masterful' and 'measured'.[4]

Dark Emu has been wildly successful and widely celebrated. But it is not true.

III

Then there is the direr case of Canada. In May 2021 an indigenous band at Kamloops, British Columbia, claimed to have discovered the remains of 215 'missing children' of an Indian Residential School. The claim was quickly sexed up by the media into a story of 'mass graves', with all its connotation of murderous atrocity. The Toronto *Globe and Mail* published an article under the title 'The Discovery of a Mass Gravesite at a Former Residential School in Kamloops Is Just the Tip of the Iceberg', in which a professor of law at UBC wrote: 'It is horrific ... a too-common unearthing of the legacy, and enduring reality, of colonialism in Canada'.[5] Prime Minister Justin Trudeau ordered Canadian flags to be flown at half-mast on all federal buildings to honour the murdered children. Because the Kamloops school had been run by Roman Catholics, some zealous citizens took to burning and vandalising churches, 112 of them to date. The dreadful tale was eagerly broadcast worldwide by Al Jazeera. It is now an established orthodoxy in Canada that these 'colonial' schools were the sites of physical atrocity and cultural genocide.

Yet, over four years after the claim was first made, not a single grave of a missing child has been discovered, because no disinterment has been attempted. What we do know is that the alleged 'mass grave' is the site of a century-old septic system, whose trenches lined with clay tiles match the direction and depth of the suspect 'sub-surface anomalies' identified by ground-penetrating radar in 2021.[6] Apart from indigenous say-so, there is no evidence of hidden graves – either in Kamloops or anywhere else in Canada.

More generally, is it true that the residential schools were forced on indigenous people? For most of their history, no. The idea originated with indigenous leaders in the 1830s, who recognised the need of their children in remote areas to adapt to the new world that had unavoidably come upon them, by learning English and agriculture. As late as the 1920s indigenous bands in Alberta and in the Northern Territory's district of Keewatin were lobbying for more such schools.[7] Parents had to apply in writing for their children to attend, since boarding was over three times more expensive than day school. And 50 per cent of indigenous children left both day and residential school after grade 1. In short, admission was only at parental request and exit was at will.[8]

It is true that in 1920 the authorities acquired the legal power to compel attendance, but that is only because all Canadian children, regardless of ethnicity, were required to go to school. And that coercive power was used sparingly. However, by the 1940s, the schools had changed their main function from being educational institutions to being care homes for native children, who had been removed from abusive, dysfunctional or simply overcrowded homes for the sake of their own welfare – sometimes with parental consent, sometimes without it.[9] That must be the period to which most contemporary testimony refers. In which case, how far memories of childhood unhappiness are due to oppressive schools, and how much to disturbed homes, must surely be a moot point.

The widespread condemnation of the residential system, however, is not confined to its last half-century. It is commonly believed that, out of a total of up to 150,000 pupils between 1883 (when the federal government started to fund residential education) and 1998 (when the last residential school closed), over 4000 died, because of culpable neglect, abuse or murder. Where does that figure come from?

Its basis is the number of deaths given in the 2015 final report of the Truth and Reconciliation Commission of Canada (TRCC): 3201. Yet, the report actually identifies only 423 named children who died on the premises of a residential school. And it admits that some, at least, of a further 409 unnamed children may be duplicates of them. It also admits that in 1391 cases (43.5 per cent) the location of death is unknown, yet it assumes that all the former pupils who died within one year of leaving did so because of poor conditions in their schools.[10]

However, records reveal that some of these died because of accidents suffered, or tuberculosis contracted, on their home reserves. Tuberculosis was a disease endemic in indigenous populations before the arrival of Europeans, and a very high proportion of children arrived at the residential schools already infected with it, because of poor living conditions at home. Even now, indigenous communities in remote areas suffer an extraordinarily high incidence of it: among non-native Canadians the current rate is 0.6 per 100,000, while among indigenous Canadians it is 24, and among the Inuit, 170. To what extent the schools inadvertently exacerbated the problem through overcrowding and poor ventilation, before reforms were made in response to Dr Bryce's reports in 1907 and 1909, is impossible to determine.[11]

The TRCC's figure of 3201 has since been inflated to 4140 by the National Centre for Truth and Reconciliation at the University of Manitoba, which claimed that the deaths had been caused by malnourishment and disease in the schools and amounted to 'atrocities'. Yet, again, that figure includes pupils who died up to a year after leaving a residential school, no matter what the cause of death, and (since 2022) the name of any pupil whose family simply wanted their attendance memorialised.[12] At least one listed was murdered months after her departure at the age of 19.[13] And another died at the ripe old age of 85.

So, how many inmates of the schools died on the premises? Assuming no duplication of the named and unnamed recorded deaths, the only firm figure is 832 or 0.55 per cent of the total of 150,000 pupils. (The death rate for non-indigenous children throughout Canada in the 1880s was 2.5 per cent.) How many indigenous children subsequently died because of poor conditions in the schools? We don't know. But we do know that many of them died from other causes or would have died from tuberculosis anyway. The claim that over three or four thousand pupils were deliberately killed or died through culpable neglect – and that their deaths amount to an 'atrocity' – is patently false, lacking any evidential basis whatsoever.

Yes, there is evidence of some sexual abuse of minors by adults at the residential schools. While lamentable, however, such misconduct is not confined to history. It happens now, and it will happen tomorrow. Sin can be contained; it cannot be abolished – not even in Canada. As for the scale of the abuse, again, we do not know. J.R. Miller, whose measured 1996 book, *Shingwauk's Vision*, is the standard history of the residential schools, observes that much of it occurred between pupils.[14] And records in the Department of Indian Affairs report the difficulty of preventing girls and boys creeping into each other's dormitories, implying that some of it, at least, was consensual.[15]

But what about the culturally 'genocidal' repression of native languages? One of the main aims of the schools was to have indigenous pupils learn English, so that they could

participate fully in the new Anglicised society that was enveloping them, and we all know that the most efficient way to
acquire a new language is to be totally immersed in it. That
said, there do appear to have been cases where the prohibi-
tion of native language-speaking was excessive. Yet, we also
know that there were schools where teachers themselves took
the trouble to learn native languages and permitted pupils to
speak them outside of the classroom.[16] The record falls a long,
long way short of systematic cultural 'genocide'.

Finally, there is the charge of inadequate funding – but
if anyone was to blame for that, they resided in Ottawa, not
in the schools themselves. Miller, for one, is scathing about
tight-fisted government bureaucrats.[17] Yet, elected governments and civil servants are more sensitive than academics
to the fact that public funds and borrowing capacity are not
infinite, and that more money spent in one direction may
well mean less spent in another. Moreover, we do need to
remember that governments in the past had nothing like the
resources they do now. As already mentioned, today in the
UK, the government has the equivalent of almost 44 per cent
of GDP at its disposal; in 1900, it had only 8 per cent. By the
1870s, the US government was spending more on fighting
frontier wars in its Wild West than the whole of the Ottawa
budget.[18] Nonetheless, in 1882 John A. MacDonald's government spent more on Indian affairs than it did on defence, the

administration of justice or civil government.[19] Was Ottawa unreasonably stingy in its expenditure on residential schools because of racist prejudice? Not obviously.

So, when all is said and done, what do we know about Canada's Indian Residential Schools? We know that conditions were invariably poor by our standards, but then so they were everywhere in the late nineteenth and early twentieth centuries – and they were often worse in the homes from which indigenous pupils came. We know that the crowding of already diseased children together and the lack of ventilation probably, although inadvertently, increased the spread of tuberculosis, until reforms were made. We know that some repression of native languages was unreasonably strict and some sexual abuse of minors by adults took place. And we know that the compulsory removal of children from dysfunctional families was distressing, notwithstanding the benevolent intention. There is, however, no firm evidence that indigenous children died in the schools in excessive numbers from culpable negligence. And there is no evidence at all of mass murder.

Nonetheless, the story of the Indian Residential Schools as sites of atrocity and genocide is now a militantly public orthodoxy in Canada – so much so that one MP has introduced a bill into the Ottawa Parliament that would criminalise Indian Residential School 'denialism'.[20] Yet the story is not true.

IV

So, prime ministers, archbishops, academics, editors and public broadcasters are all in the business of exaggerating the colonial sins of their own countries against noble (not-so-very) savages – from London to Sydney to Toronto. Why?

An obvious reason is the admirable and well-meaning inclination to correct racial injustices and so to 'heal' race relations. Accordingly, for example, the Church Commissioners of the Church of England declare: 'We believe every person is created in God's image. New Testament teaching is focussed on God's desire for human beings to live in harmony. Justice, in this case racial justice, must be part of, not distinct from, biblical theology and, hence, the Church Commissioners' work.'[21] But that does not explain the reckless, dismissive brushing aside of concerns about the truth in the eager (or desperate) rush to confess imaginary sins and do penance for them.

From Canada comes evidence that part of the problem is a press intent on attracting attention (and subscriptions) in a highly competitive media market. Even back in the 1990s, Miller observed that a sensation-seeking media had an appetite only for stories of abuse and horror. Positive testimony from former pupils at the Indian Residential Schools was denied column inches.[22]

Financial interests have also been at work. A compensation system in Canada offered considerable sums to any former pupil claiming to have suffered abuse, without subjecting the claim to much or any kind of testing. Given universal human nature, it is a practical certainty that many such claims were exaggerated or fabricated and that the negative bias of the public record was further exacerbated. Money is also, of course, a leading motive for CARICOM's claims of reparations for slavery.

In the case of the Church of England, there is the desire of the leaders of a historic institution to broaden its shrinking popular appeal and recover the leading social role it once played. 'We believe that by addressing our past transparently ... the Church and its teachings will be more relevant to more people ...', declare the Commissioners. 'Visibly demonstrating that the Church of England is for all will help to make it more relevant to more people across our nation ...'.[23] Moreover, 'we believe we are enabling the Church Commissioners to fulfil part of its mission: to revitalise the Church and to be faithful to Christ's calling to play a leading role in building a society rooted in justice and compassion'.[24] These motives are perfectly legitimate, of course, but not when desperation drives them to trample over the truth.

V

This desire for the recovery of national leadership by the Church of England also finds expression in Michael Banner's book *Britain's Slavery Debt*. Here, after methodically articulating an apologia for slavery reparations entirely lacking in the Church Commissioners' documents, Banner holds out the hope that the Church will lead other British national institutions in repenting of its historic sins and making amends for them. He makes clear, however, that reparations are not only about doing justice to the descendants of slaves in the Caribbean; they are also about the British exorcising their continuing racism. The preface to his book makes clear the author's conviction that the British are systemically racist, and that this racism stems directly from colonialism and its epitome, slavery.

Banner takes this view mainly because of his own experience. 'My personal failing reflects a national failing', he confesses.[25] In the forty years prior to 2007, in the heart of which the young Michael was growing up, 'everyday racism' was 'very much the norm', he tells us, and 'ubiquitous'.[26] Enoch Powell – he of the infamous 'rivers of blood' speech against mass immigration – 'was the most popular politician of his day and was spoken of not as a pariah but as a voice in the wilderness'.[27] Concern about Rhodesia and South Africa

was focused 'definitely not [upon] the plights of their major-
ities but of their minorities in staving off majority rule'. And
an Iranian friend at a leading public school reported that he
was routinely addressed as a 'w*g'.[28]

I cannot speak for Michael Banner and the circles in
which he grew up – slightly later than I. And I do not deny
that racial prejudice was present in Britain in the second half
of the twentieth century. But I do assert that anti-racism was
also vigorously present. Powell's 'rivers of blood' speech was
immediately and fiercely controversial and it ended his political career. He was regarded, of course, as *both* a voice in the
wilderness *and* a pariah by different people. And, yes, there
was natural concern about what would become of whites in
democratised, black-majority southern Africa. But at the
same time, the anti-Apartheid movement in Britain enjoyed
considerable public support. Racial prejudice was not as
all-pervasive as Banner would have us believe. After all, four
years after he was born Parliament passed the Race Relations
Act 1965, which outlawed racial discrimination. Of course,
that does imply that there was a racist problem. But it also
implies that there was a prevailing anti-racist will to realise
a solution. And, as it happens, I, too, had an Anglo-Iranian
friend at my public school, whose name and features marked
him out and who had a Persian text in Arabic script pinned
up ostentatiously above his desk. I never once witnessed him

suffer, or heard him complain of, racial abuse and I am confident that, had he ever been subjected to it, his peers would have protested vigorously.

So why does Banner presume to project his own personal sense of guilt onto the national stage? Why does he paint the national picture in needlessly dark colours? Why is his reading about his own country's colonial record and involvement in slavery confined to a casual handful of left-wing sources? I have no insight into his soul, of course, and I shall not speculate about it. But I observe that his bias is typical of his social class as a senior Anglican clergyman and Cambridge University ethicist: English, university-educated and intellectual. That is my class, too, and I know it well. And among the things that my 'lived experience' has taught me is that it typically considers patriotism to be vulgar at best, and at worst 'fascist'. Or to be more exact, it disdains English or British patriotism, but not Irish or Scottish nationalism – because they are anti-British. It regards its own national self-transcendence as a mark of its moral superiority.

It seems that this is no new phenomenon, for George Orwell identified it over eighty years ago in 1941:

In the general patriotism of the country they [the English intelligentsia] form a sort of island of dissident thought. England is perhaps the only great country whose intellectuals are ashamed of their own nationality. In left-wing circles, it is always felt that there is something slightly disgraceful in being an Englishman and that it is a duty to snigger at every English institution ... It is a strange fact, but it is unquestionably true that almost any English intellectual would feel more ashamed of standing to attention during 'God save the King' than of stealing from a poor box. All through the critical years [of the Second World War] many left-wingers were chipping away at English morale, trying to spread an outlook that was sometimes squashily pacifist, sometimes violently pro-Russian, but always anti-British.[29]

The proper complaint is not at all that intellectuals are critical of their own country: countries, not being divine and being made up of fallible creatures and sinners, often deserve criticism. No, the proper complaint is that intellectuals' criticism is entirely unrestrained by any sense of gratitude or loyalty towards the country that enables them to lead their privileged lives. They speak of it as if it had nothing to do with them, as if it were alien. That is why they are so cavalier with their criticism – because, not identifying with its target, they feel no pain in making it. They cheerfully bite the national hand that feeds them, carelessly over-egging its sins and trashing its history, because they do not consider it their own.

Which has led me to wonder – though I cannot prove it – whether the present tendency to rub British noses in exaggerated guilt over slavery and racism is partly Remainers' revenge for Brexit. That is why my attention sharpened when I noticed that, immediately before the passage quoted above, George Orwell wrote this: 'the English intelligentsia are Europeanized. They take their cookery from Paris and their opinions from Moscow.'[30]

VI

The social habit of careless, ungrateful anti-British prejudice goes some way towards explaining the rush to condemn. Yet that requires explanation, too. Here, I think we must reach for spiritual terms – that is, terms that talk of how human beings try to endow their little, transient lives with larger, more lasting significance. I read the anti-patriotism of the English intellectual as the expression of a degenerate Christian sensibility.

For Christians, the paradoxical mark of the genuinely righteous person is a profound awareness of their own unrighteousness. The saint stands out as one who knows more deeply than others just what a sinner she really is. There is much virtue in this, of course, for it tempers self-righteousness with compassion for fellow sinners, forbidding the righteous to cast the unrighteous beyond the human pale. Yet, like all virtue, it can be corrupted and turn into vice. As Jesus pointed out, humility can be infected by pride – or, more precisely, by public virtue-signalling.[31] For genuine humility can degenerate into a perverse bid for supreme self-righteousness, which exaggerates one's sins and broadcasts the display of repentance: holier-than-thou because more-sinful-than-thou. In *The Tyranny of Guilt: An Essay on Western Masochism* (first published in French in 2006), the French philosopher Pascal Bruckner captures this when he writes of contemporary, post-imperial Europe (and, by extension, the West):

> This is the paternalism of the guilty conscience: seeing ourselves as the kings of infamy is still a way of staying on the crest of history ... Europe is still messianic in a minor key ... Barbarity is Europe's great pride, which it acknowledges only in itself; it denies that others are barbarous, finding attenuating circumstances for them (which is a way of denying them all responsibility).[32]

In this self-regarding display of virtue, the penitent hogs the stage: 'by erecting lack of love for oneself into a leading principle, we lie to ourselves about ourselves and close ourselves to others . . . In Western self-hatred, the Other has no place. It is a narcissistic relationship in which the African, the Indian, and Arab are brought in as extras.'[33]

If this is the malaise, what is the cure? Certainly, less of the existential anxiety that drives mortal human creatures to pretend to immortal divinity by puffing up their saintly virtue. To that end, more religious faith would help, since a great advantage of believing in a God is that the believer is less likely to mistake himself for one. Moreover, those who find the loving eye of God sufficient can cope without the adoring eye of the world. They are content to be the hidden faithful, spiritually free to concentrate on doing good rather than appearing virtuous, of whom George Eliot wrote so memorably: 'the growing good of the world is partly dependent on unhistoric acts; and that things are not so ill with you and me as they might have been, is half owing to the number who lived faithfully a hidden life, and rest in unvisited tombs'.[34]

Such modest, genuine saints will not waste their time loudly proclaiming their 'anti-racism' in defiance of the historical truth about slavery and the empirical truth about racism today. Rather, they will be intent upon diagnosing its actual causes in the light of all the evidence, in order to craft an effective remedy. Because they care more about solving the problem than signalling their virtue.

NOTES

PREFACE

1 Elie Kedourie, *In the Anglo-Arab Labyrinth: The McMahon-Husayn Correspondence and Its Interpretations, 1914–1939*, 2nd edn (London: Frank Cass, 2000), p.220.

2 Michelle Stirling, 'Mark Carney's Disturbing Silence on Residential School Genocide Claims', *Western Standard*, 6 May 2023: https://www.westernstandard.news/opinion/stirling-mark-carneys-disturbing-silence-on-residential-school-genocide-claims/article_1407e424-eb88-11ed-87d0-efa1f4364759.html (accessed 11 April 2025).

3 Nigel Biggar, 'Schools Were No "Atrocity". Just Look at the Evidence', *National Post*, 2 April 2025: https://nationalpost.com/opinion/nigel-biggar-residential-schools-were-no-atrocity-just-look-at-the-evidence (accessed 11 April 2025).

1 INTRODUCTION: WHY NOW?

1 'CARICOM' denotes the 'Caribbean Community', a political and economic organisation of fifteen member states and five associates.

2 CARICOM, 'Reparations for Native Genocide and Slavery', 13 October 2015: https://caricom.org/reparations-for-native-genocide-and-slavery/ (accessed 4 April 2025).

3 Coleman Bazelon, Alberto Vargas, Rohan Janakiraman and Mary M. Olson, *Quantification of Reparations for Transatlantic Chattel Slavery* (New York: Brattle Group, 8 June 2023): https://www.brattle.com/wp-content/uploads/2023/07/Report-on-Reparations-for-Transatlantic-Chattel-Slavery-in-the-Americas-and-the-Caribbean.pdf (accessed 21 March 2025), pp 4, 81, table 35.

4 Greg Heffer, 'Labour MPs Demand Britain Pays Reparations to

Caribbean Countries for Slave Trade and "400 Years of Hideous Abuse"', *Mail*, 10 March 2023: https://www.dailymail.co.uk/news/article-11839257/Labour-MPs-demand-Britain-pays-reparations-Caribbean-countries-400-years-hideous-abuse.html (accessed 21 March 2025).

5 Craig Simpson, 'Caribbean Lobbyists Funded by Telecoms Billionaire Draft "Bespoke" Reparations Plans', *Telegraph*, 10 September 2023: https://www.telegraph.co.uk/news/2023/09/10/caribbean-lobbyists-billionaire-funding-reparations-demand/ (accessed 21 March 2023).

6 Ronald Niezen, *The Origins of Indigenism: Human Rights and the Politics of Identity* (Berkeley, CA: University of California Press, 2003), ch.2.

7 United Nations Declaration on the Rights of Indigenous Peoples, 13 September 2007: https://www.ohchr.org/sites/default/files/Documents/Publications/Declaration_indigenous_en.pdf (accessed 21 March 2025).

8 European Union Agency for Fundamental Rights, *Being Black in the EU: Summary of the Second European Union Minorities and Discrimination Survey* (Vienna: EUAFR, 2019): https://fra.europa.eu/sites/default/files/fra_uploads/fra-2019-being-black-in-the-eu-summary_en.pdf (accessed 21 March 2025), pp 2, 3, 7, 9.

9 Commission on Race and Ethnic Disparities (CRED), *The Report* (London: HMSO, 2021): https://assets.publishing.service.gov.uk/media/6062ddb1d3bf7f5ce1060aa4/20210331_-_CRED_Report_-_FINAL_-_Web_Accessible.pdf (accessed 21 March 2025), pp 8, 36, 77.

10 ibid., pp 8–9.

11 ibid., p.55.

12 ibid., p.71.

13 ibid., p.110.

14 ibid., p.32.

15 Rob Lownie, 'Survey: UK Is One of the Least Racist Countries in the World', *Unherd*, 27 April 2023: https://unherd.com/newsroom/survey-uk-is-one-of-the-least-racist-countries-in-the-world/ (accessed 21 March 2025). This refers to Suzanne Hall et al., *Love Thy Neighbour? Public Trust and Acceptance of the People Who Live Alongside Us*, the UK in the World Values Survey (London: Policy Institute at King's College London, April 2023): https://www.kcl.ac.uk/policy-institute/assets/love-thy-neighbour.pdf (accessed 21 March 2025).

2 JUDGING THE PAST

1 Denis O'Brien, letter, *Sunday Telegraph*, 9 February 2025.

2 G.H. Le May, *British Supremacy in South Africa, 1899–1907* (Oxford: Clarendon Press, 1965), p.57.

3 Yves R. Simon, *The Ethiopian Campaign and French Political Thought*, ed. Anthony O. Simon, trans. Robert Royal (Notre Dame: University of Notre Dame, 2009), p.55.

4 Reinhold Niebuhr (1892–1971) was an American Protestant theologian and public intellectual.

3 CONTEXT 1: SLAVERY'S UNIVERSALITY

1 G.B. Pyrah, *Imperial Policy and South Africa, 1902–10* (Oxford: Clarendon Press, 1955), p.191.

2 Bridglal Pachai, 'Indentured Chinese Immigrant Labour on the Witwatersrand Goldfields', *India Quarterly*, 21/1 (January–March 1965), pp 59, 65.

3 Peter Richardson, 'The Recruiting of Chinese Indentured Labour for the South African Gold Mines, 1903–1908', *Journal of African History*, 18/1 (1977), p.86.

4 Pachai, 'Indentured Chinese Immigrant Labour', p.69.

5 ibid., p.80. According to Kartar Lalvani, it is also estimated that of the more than 150,000 indentured male labourers who had arrived in South Africa from India since 1860, only a quarter opted to return home: *The Making of India: The Untold Story of British Enterprise* (London: Bloomsbury, 2016), p.396. And according to Orlando Patterson, only one third of Indians who came as indentured labourers to Jamaica returned home: 'Why Has Jamaica Trailed Barbados on the Path to Sustained Growth? The Role of Institutions, Colonialism, and Cultural Appropriation', in *The Confounding Island: Jamaica and the Postcolonial Predicament* (Cambridge, MA: Belknap Press, 2019), p.50.

6 Niall Ferguson, *Empire: How Britain Made the Modern World* (London: Allen Lane, 2003), p.74.

7 Patterson, 'Why Has Jamaica Trailed Barbados', p.46.

8 For an analysis of the differences between indentured servitude and

slavery, see Jerome S. Handler and Matthew C. Reilly, 'Contesting "White Slavery" in the Caribbean: Enslaved Africans and European Indentured Servants in Seventeenth-Century Barbados', *New West Indian Guide*, 91 (2017), esp. pp 38–45.

9   Jonathan A.C. Brown bravely conducts an original and searching analysis of the moral wrongness of 'slavery' in *Slavery and Islam* (London: Oneworld Academic, 2019), pp 15–65, 147–200.

10 This piece of historically informed fiction is imagined by Brown in ibid., pp 28–9, and based on Shaun Marmon, 'Domestic Slavery in the Mamluk Empire: A Preliminary Sketch', in Shaun Marmon (ed.), *Slavery in the Islamic Middle East* (Princeton, NJ: Markus Wiener, 1999).

11 Brown, *Slavery and Islam*, pp 29–30; see also G. Veinstein, 'Soḳullu Meḥmed Pasha', in P. Bearman, T. Bianquis, C.E. Bosworth, E. van Donzel and W.P. Heinrichs (eds), *Encyclopaedia of Islam*, 2nd edn (Leiden: Brill, 2012).

12 National Park Service, 'Andersonville: The Deadly Confederate Prison Camp': https://www.battlefields.org/learn/articles/andersonville-prison (accessed 20 February 2025).

13 David Eltis, *The Rise of African Slavery in the Americas* (Cambridge: Cambridge University Press, 2000), p.65.

14 David Ritchie, *Natural Rights: A Criticism of Some Ethical and Political Conceptions* (London: Swan Sonnenschein, 1895), p.104.

15 See Leland Donald, *Aboriginal Slavery on the Northwest Coast of North America* (Berkeley and Los Angeles, CA: University of California Press, 1997), and Ted Binnema, *The Vancouver Island Treaties and the Evolving Principles of Indigenous Title* (Toronto: University of Toronto, 2025).

16 Pekka Hämäläinen, *The Comanche Empire* (New Haven, CT, and London: Yale University Press, 2008), p.14.

17 Robert C. Davis, *Christian Slaves, Muslim Masters: White Slavery in the Mediterranean, the Barbary Coast and Italy, 1500–1800* (London: Palgrave Macmillan, 2003). These figures do not include Europeans enslaved by other Mediterranean traders – for example, those based in Morocco. Davis's calculations are not based on records, which do not exist, but on what would be needed to replenish the slave population, given annual losses to death, escape, ransom and conversion to Islam. His unavoidably speculative conclusion has been met with some

scepticism, for example, from Peter Earle, author of *Corsairs of Malta and Barbary* (London: Sidgwick and Jackson, 1970), and John Wright in *The Trans-Saharan Slave Trade* (London: Routledge, 2007). See Rory Carroll, 'New Book Reopens Old Arguments about Slave Raids on Europe', *Guardian*, 11 March 2004: https://www.theguardian.com/uk/2004/mar/11/highereducation.books (accessed 4 April 2025).

18 See Olivier Pétré-Grenouilleau, *Les traites négrières: essai d'histoire globale* (Paris: Editions Gallimard, 2004). Pétré-Grenouilleau has been described as 'one of the most . . . distinguished historians in France': Joseph C. Miller, 'A Global History of the Slave Trade', *Journal of African History*, 49/2 (2008), p.306. His book won the Prix de l'Essai de l'Académie Française and the Livre d'Histoire prize of the Senate of the French Republic.

19 Justin Marozzi, *Captives and Companions: A History of Slavery and the Slave Trade in the Islamic World* (London: Penguin, 2025), excerpt from the publisher's summary description online: https://www.penguin.co.uk/books/444740/captives-and-companions-by-marozzi-justin/9780241522158 (accessed 3 May 2025). Pages that substantiate the claims include pp 6–7, 7–8, 397–8, 401–2, 404.

4 BRITISH SLAVERY

1 David Pelteret, *Slavery in Early Medieval England: From the Reign of Alfred to the Twelfth Century* (Woodbridge: Boydell Press, 1995).

2 Michael Tugendhat, 'Human Rights in Britain and France from Thomas Becket to the French Revolution', Inner Temple History Society Lecture, London, 10 October 2022: https://www.innertemple.org.uk/education/education-resources/history-society-lecture-recordings/human-rights-in-britain-and-france/ (accessed 4 April 2025).

3 Stephen D. Behrendt, 'The Transatlantic Slave Trade', in Robert L. Paquette and Mark M. Smith (eds), *The Oxford Handbook of Slavery in the Americas* (Oxford: Oxford University Press, 2010), p.262, table 11.1. David Richardson reports a slightly higher figure of over 3.4 million slaves exported by the British from Africa in the shorter period of 1662–1807: 'The British Empire and the Atlantic Slave Trade, 1660–1807', in Roger W. Louis (ed.), *The Oxford History of the British Empire*,

5 vols (Oxford: Oxford University Press, 1999), vol.ii: 'The Eighteenth Century', ed. P.J. Marshall, p.441.

4   Frank Kitson, *Prince Rupert: Admiral and General-at-Sea* (London: Constable, 1999), p.238. The Royal African Company was founded in 1672 but had its origins in the Company of Royal Adventurers Trading into Africa, which had been established in 1660.

5   Olaudah Equiano, *The Interesting Narrative and Other Writings*, ed. Vincent Carretta, rev. edn (New York: Penguin, 2003), p.58; quoted by Adam Hochschild, *Bury the Chains: The British Struggle to Abolish Slavery* (London: Macmillan, 2005), p.32. The truthfulness of Equiano's testimony is a matter of dispute. Documentary evidence has been unearthed that states that he was born, not in Africa, but in South Carolina. If so, his description of transportation cannot be based on first-hand experience. Nonetheless, it could still be an accurate rendition of what he learned of others' direct experience. See Vincent Carretta, *Equiano, the African: Biography of a Self-Made Man* (Athens: University of Georgia Press, 2005).

6   Behrendt, 'The Transatlantic Slave Trade', p.260; citing Philip D. Curtin's *The Atlantic Slave Trade: A Census* (Madison, WI: University of Wisconsin Press, 1969).

7   In 1788 Jamaica's assembly passed the Consolidated Slave Law, which was intended to keep families together: Kenneth Morgan, *Slavery and the British Empire: From Africa to America* (Oxford: Oxford University Press, 2007), p.77.

8   Larry Gragg, *Englishmen Transplanted: The English Colonization of Barbados, 1627–1660* (Oxford: Oxford University Press, 2003), p.129.

9   Morgan Godwyn, *The Negro's & Indians Advocate, Suing for Their Admission into the Church* ... (London, 1680), quoted in Alden T. Vaughan, *Roots of American Racism: Essays on the Colonial Experience* (Oxford: Oxford University Press, 1995), p.72.

10 Michael Craton, *Testing the Chains: Resistance to Slavery in the British West Indies* (Ithaca, NY: Cornell University Press, 1982), pp 109–10.

11 Morgan, *Slavery and the British Empire*, p.137.

12 Thomas Thistlewood, Folder 38, Box 7, Thomas Thistlewood Papers, James Marshall and Marie-Louise Osborn Collection, Beinecke Rare Book and Manuscript Library, Yale University; quoted by Helen McKee, 'From Violence to Alliance: Maroons and White Settlers in

Jamaica, 1739–1795', *Slavery and Abolition*, 39/1 (2018), p.39.

13 Morgan, *Slavery and the British Empire*, pp 23–4, 113. See also Handler and Reilly, 'Contesting "White Slavery" in the Caribbean', pp 38–45.

14 Mohammed Bashir Salau, *Sokoto Caliphate: A Historical and Comparative Study*, Rochester Studies in African History and the Diaspora, vol.80 (Martlesham: Boydell & Brewer, 2019), p.21.

15 ibid., p.143.

16 Jan S. Hogendorn and Paul E. Lovejoy, *Slow Death for Slavery. The Course of Abolition in Northern Nigeria, 1897–1936* (Cambridge: Cambridge University Press, 1993), pp xiii, 1.

17 Salau, *Sokoto Caliphate*, p.161.

18 See Nigel Biggar, *Colonialism: A Moral Reckoning* (London: William Collins, 2023, 2024), pp 48–51.

19 Christopher de Bellaigue, *The Golden Throne: The Curse of a King* (London: Bodley Head, 2025), p.24.

20 Davis, *Christian Slaves, Muslim Masters*, p.69; quoting Henri-David de Grammont, *La course, l'esclavage et la redemption à Alger*, Etudes algériennes (Paris, 1885), p.53 (not p.11, as Davis reports): 'Il pouvait le revendre, le surcharger de travail, l'emprisonner, le frapper, le mutiler, le tuer, sans que personne s'en mélât'.

21 Antonio de Sosa, *Topography of Algiers: Attempted Escape of Miguel de Cervantes* (*c.*1577), in Mario Klarer (ed.), *Barbary Captives: An Anthology of Early Modern Slave Memoirs by Europeans in North Africa* (New York: Columbia University Press, 2022), p.97. De Sosa was a fellow captive with Cervantes.

22 According to the database of the Slave Voyages project: https://www. slavevoyages.org/assessment/estimates (accessed 9 June 2025).

23 Eric Williams, *Capitalism and Slavery* (Chapel Hill, NC: University of North Carolina Press, 1944), p.105.

24 ibid., pp 105–6.

25 Roger Anstey, 'Capitalism and Slavery: A Critique', *The Economic History Review*, new series, 21/2 (August 1968).

26 Richardson, 'The British Empire and the Atlantic Slave Trade', p.461. C.H. Feinstein argues that 'the economic profits of the [slave] trade were merely wasted in Africa, not funnelled into industry in Britain': 'Capital Accumulation and the Industrial Revolution', in Roderick Floud and Donald McCloskey (eds), *The Economic History of Britain*

since 1700, 1st edn, 2 vols (Cambridge: Cambridge University Press, 1981), vol.i, pp 99–100.

27 David Eltis and Stanley L. Engerman, 'The Importance of Slavery and the Slave Trade to Industrializing Britain', *Journal of Economic History*, 60/1 (March 2000), p.130. I thank Professor Doug Stokes for drawing my attention to this quotation: 'Did Slavery Make Britain Rich?', *Doug's Newsletter*, 23 October 2022: https://dougstokes.substack.com/p/did-slavery-make-britain-rich#_ftnref16 (accessed 1 April 2025).

28 David Brion Davis, 'Foreword', in Seymour Drescher, *Econocide: British Slavery in the Era of Abolition*, 2nd edn (Chapel Hill, NC: University of North Carolina Press, 2010), p.xiv.

29 According to David Eltis and Stanley L. Engerman, one expression of this view is Robin Blackburn's *The Making of New World Slavery: From the Baroque to the Modern, 1492–1800* (London: Verso, 1997). See Eltis and Engerman, 'The Importance of Slavery', p.124.

30 ibid., p.135.

31 Joel Mokyr, 'Editor's Introduction: The New Economic History and the Industrial Revolution', in Joel Mokyr (ed.), *The British Industrial Revolution: An Economic Perspective*, 2nd edn (London: Routledge, 1999), pp 49–50. According to Lawrence Goldman and Robert Tombs, in 'The Church of England's Historic Links to the Transatlantic Slave Trade', *History Reclaimed*, 1 July 2024: 'The Williams Thesis minimised the complex range of factors that played significant parts in industrialising Britain, and it has been contradicted by substantial scholarship carried out since the 1940s. Enlightenment thought and scientific discovery [Joel Mokyr, *The Enlightened Economy: An Economic History of Britain 1700–1850* (New Haven, CT: Yale University Press, 2012)], pre-existing economic development [R.C. Allen, 'Why the Industrial Revolution was British: Commerce, Induced Invention, and the Scientific Revolution', *The Economic History Review*, 64/2 (May 2011), p.358], cheap mineral fuel [E.A. Wrigley, *Energy and the English Industrial Revolution* (Cambridge: Cambridge University Press, 2015), p.4], and industrial innovation are dismissed or simply ignored by "decolonialist" followers of the Williams Thesis, who attribute the rise of the West to slavery and the slave trade [e.g., Kehinde Andrews, *The New Age of Empire: How Racism and Colonialism Still Rule the World* (London: Penguin Books,

2022); Sathnam Sanghera, *Empireland: How Imperialism Has Shaped Modern Britain* (London: Penguin Books, 2021); Priyamvada Gopal, *Insurgent Empire: Anticolonial Resistance and British Dissent* (London: Verso, 2019)]'. See https://historyreclaimed.co.uk/the-church-of-englands-historic-links-to-the-transatlantic-slave-trade/ (accessed 1 April 2025).

32 Morgan, *Slavery and the British Empire*, p.83.

33 Maxine Berg and Pat Hudson, *Slavery, Capitalism, and the Industrial Revolution* (London: Polity, 2023), pp 58, 191.

34 ibid., p.7.

35 See T.S. Ashton, *The Industrial Revolution 1760–1830* (Oxford: Oxford University Press, 1997).

36 ibid., pp 220–21; Tirthankar Roy, in a tweet dated 13 October 2023: '"Trade between Britain, Africa and the Americas is often referred to as a triangular trade. The model might be viewed as a diamond-shaped trade that integrated the Indian and Atlantic Oceans." Yes, but this radical claim rests unsteadily on one product, Indian textiles.'

37 Berg and Hudson, *Slavery*, p.21.

38 ibid., p.52.

39 ibid., p.7.

40 While Berg and Hudson are economic historians of good academic repute, both the content of their book and the timing of its publication indicate that it was written in support of advocacy for reparations for historic slavery. Especially in the penultimate chapter (9), 'Slavery after Slavery: Legacies of Race and Inequality', the authors stray far beyond their professional expertise into the sociology of race and inequality in contemporary Britain and into the ethics of 'restorative justice'. Further, their political partisanship is revealed in that they write about these issues as if there were only one point of view. Thus, they appeal to the Runnymede Trust's report (p.204n.88), while ignoring that of the 'Sewell' Commission on Race and Ethnic Diversity; and they invoke Daniel Butt in favour of restorative justice (p.204n.90), while ignoring arguments against reparations made by Onora O'Neill and Jeremy Waldron. They also cite the unreliable Hilary Beckles liberally and uncritically (ch.9, throughout the footnotes).

41 David Eltis, *Atlantic Cataclysm: Rethinking the Atlantic Slave Trades* (Cambridge: Cambridge University Press, 2024), back cover.

42 ibid., pp 145–7.
43 ibid., p.360.
44 ibid., p.150.
45 ibid., p.360.
46 ibid., p.361.
47 ibid., back cover.
48 ibid., p.147.

5 CONTEXT 2: AFRICAN COMPLICITY

1   Michael Banner, *Britain's Slavery Debt: Reparations Now!* (Oxford: Oxford University Press, 2024), p.15.
2   Hilary M. Beckles, *Britain's Black Debt: Reparations for Caribbean Slavery and Native Genocide* (Kingston, Jamaica: University of West Indies Press, 2013), p.168.
3   For example, by Nora Wittmann, 'Examining (Il)Legality of Transatlantic Chattel Slavery: African Law', in Justine Stefanelli and Erin Lovall (eds), *Reparations under International Law for Enslavement of African Persons in the Americas and the Caribbean*, Proceedings of the Symposium of 20–21 May 2021, co-sponsored by the American Society of International Law and the Office of the Vice-Chancellor, the University of the West Indies (Washington, DC: American Society of International Law, 2022), p.34.
4   Adam Hochschild, *King Leopold's Ghost: A Story of Greed, Terror, and Heroism in Colonial Africa* (New York: Houghton Mifflin Harcourt Publishing, 2020), pp 15–16; citing Affonso I, *Correspondence de Dom Affonso, roi du Congo, 1506–43*, ed. Louis Jadin and Mireille Decorato (Brussels: Académie Royale des Sciences d'Outre Mer, 1974), pp 156, 167.
5   For a summary of the historiographical controversy, see Linda M. Heywood, 'Slavery and Its Transformation in the Kingdom of Kongo, 1491–1800', *Journal of African History*, 50/1 (2009), pp 1–2.
6   John Thornton, 'African Political Ethics and the Slave Trade', in Derek R. Peterson (ed.), *Abolitionism and Imperialism in Britain, Africa, and the Atlantic* (Athens, OH: University of Athens Press, 2010), p.40. Those against whom Thornton argues are Anne Hilton and, depending on Hilton, Joseph E. Inikori. See Hilton's *The Kingdom of Kongo* (Oxford: Oxford University Press, 1985) and Inikori's 'Slavery

in Africa and the Transatlantic Slave Trade', in Alusine Jalloh and Stephen E. Maizlish (eds), *The African Diaspora* (College Station, TX: Texas A&M University Press, 1966).

7   Thornton, 'African Political Ethics', pp 41–2.

8   ibid., p.45.

9   ibid., p.46.

10 ibid., p.53.

11 ibid., p.60n.37.

12 Heywood, 'Slavery and Its Transformation', pp 1, 3.

13 'Historian: "Africans Must Be Condemned for the Slave Trade"', interview with Abiola Félix Iroko on Benin Web TV, *Free West Media*, 28 July 2020: https://freewestmedia.com/2020/07/28/historian-africans-must-be-condemned-for-the-slave-trade/ (accessed 29 June 2021).

14 John Iliffe, *Africans: The History of a Continent*, 3rd edn (Cambridge: Cambridge University Press, 2017), p.159. In the second edition of their *Atlas of the Transatlantic Slave Trade* (New Haven: Yale University Press, 2025), David Eltis and David Richardson use figures derived from their transatlantic slave trade database, www.slavevoyages.org, to present maps showing the traffic between modern countries in Africa and those in the Americas. This would provide a numerical basis for estimating the reparations due from Africa to the countries to which slaves were sent – if anyone were minded to mount a campaign.

15 N. Levtzion and J.F.P. Hopkins (eds), *Corpus of Early Arabic Sources for West African History* (Cambridge: Cambridge University Press, 1981), p.52.

16 Robin Law, 'Human Sacrifice in Pre-Colonial Africa', *African Affairs*, 84/334 (January 1985), esp. pp 57–8, 60, 61, 62, 70, 73, 74. See also Stephen D. Behrendt, A.J.H. Latham and David A. Northrup, *The Diary of Antera Duke, an Eighteenth-Century African Slave Trader* (New York: Oxford University Press, 2010), pp 8, 28, 29, 37, 38, 251n.87.

17 J.D. Fage, 'African Societies and the Atlantic Slave Trade', *Past and Present*, cxxv (1989), pp 97–115.

18 Walter Rodney, 'African Slavery and Other Forms of Social Oppression on the Upper Guinea Coast in the Context of the Atlantic Slave Trade', *Journal of African History*, 7/3 (1966), p.443: 'many of the forms of slavery and subjection present in Africa in the nineteenth and twentieth centuries and considered indigenous to that

continent were in reality engendered by the Atlantic slave trade'.

19 Richardson, 'The British Empire and the Atlantic Slave Trade', p.463.
20 Thornton, 'African Political Ethics', pp 55–6.

6 CONTEXT 3: BRITISH ABOLITION

1 James Somerset was an African slave, who was brought from Boston, Massachusetts, to England by his owner, Charles Stewart, in 1769. In 1771 Somerset escaped but was captured shortly thereafter and imprisoned on a ship bound for Jamaica. Before the ship departed, however, Somerset's three English godparents applied to the Court of the King's Bench for his release. In his judgement of the case on 22 June 1772, Lord Mansfield concluded thus:

> The power of a master over his slave has been extremely different, in different countries. The state of slavery is of such a nature, that it is incapable of being introduced on any reasons, moral or political; but only positive law, which preserves its force long after the reasons, occasion, and time itself from whence it was created, is erased from memory: it's so odious, that nothing can be suffered to support it, but positive law. Whatever inconveniences, therefore, may follow from a decision, I cannot say this case is allowed or approved by the law of England; and therefore the black must be discharged.

http://www.commonlii.org/int/cases/EngR/1772/57.pdf

2 McKee, 'From Violence to Alliance', p.28.
3 Mavis C. Campbell, *The Maroons of Jamaica, 1655–1796* (Granby, MA: Bergin and Garvin, 1988), pp 198–9.
4 Sudhir Hazareesingh, *Black Spartacus: The Epic Life of Toussaint Louverture* (London: Allen Lane, 2020), pp 9, 30–31.
5 David Eltis reports:

> [Thomas] Haskell has listed preconditions for the historical emergence of humanitarianism as, first, an ethical maxim that makes the alleviation of suffering right, second, a sense of being causally involved in the situation that gives rise to the suffering,

and, lastly, possession of a recipe for intervention so easily applied that refusal to employ it might be considered 'an intentional act in itself'. The market system peculiar to the late eigthteenth century North Atlantic world 'expanded the range of causal perception and inspired people's confidence to intervene'.

Eltis, *Rise of African Slavery*, p.80. See also ibid., 'Epilogue on Abolition', pp 281–3.

6   See, for example, John D.O. Fulton, *Slavery and the Scottish Enlightenment* (Stroud: Fonthill Media, 2024).

7   Charles Louis de Secondat, Baron de Montesquieu, *The Complete Works of M. de Montesquieu*, 4 vols (London: T. Evans, 1777), vol.i: 'The Spirit of Laws', Book xv, ch.1, p.311.

8   Adam Smith, *The Theory of Moral Sentiments*, ed. Dugald Stewart (London: Henry G. Bohn, 1853), Part v, ch.2, p.299. It seems that Smith was not alone in taking a romantic view of Africans. Kenneth Morgan refers to a 'stream of popular works [that] upheld the primitivism of Negroes as something to be admired for its simplicity, sincerity, and lack of worldly vices': *Slavery and the British Empire*, p.159.

9   John Wesley, *Thoughts Upon Slavery* (London and Philadelphia, PA: John Cruckshank, 1774), title page and p.56.

10 Equiano, *The Interesting Narrative*.

11 The Clapham Sect was a network of socially and politically prominent evangelical Anglicans who laboured for various social reforms, including the abolition of slavery, from the 1780s to the 1840s. Many of them worshipped at Holy Trinity Church on Clapham Common, London. Hence the name.

12 John Stauffer, 'Abolition and Antislavery', in Paquette and Smith (eds), *The Oxford Handbook of Slavery in the Americas*, p.564.

13 ibid., p.563.

14 Morgan, *Slavery and the British Empire*, pp 178–81.

15 16 March 1824, House of Commons, cited in George R. Mellor, *British Imperial Trusteeship, 1783–1850* (London: Faber & Faber, 1951), p.92. Nevertheless, the London government did consider suspending Jamaica's constitution and imposing direct Crown colony rule in 1838.

16 Howick to the Earl of Mulgrave, 7 July 1832; quoted by Hochschild in *Bury the Chains*, p.344.

17 Roger Anstey, *The Atlantic Slave Trade and British Abolition, 1760–1810* (London: Macmillan, 1975), pp 51–3.

18 Davis, 'Foreword', p.xv.

19 For a summary of the historical debate provoked by Eric Williams's *Capitalism and Slavery*, see Gad Heuman, 'Slavery, the Slave Trade, and Abolition', in Louis (ed.), *The Oxford History of the British Empire*, vol.v: 'Historiography', ed. Robin Winks, pp 322–4. In this section I have relied heavily on Morgan, *Slavery and the British Empire*, pp 191–2, 194–8, supplemented by Jeremy Black, *Slavery: A New Global History* (London: Constable and Robinson, 2011), p.216.

20 Thomas Clarkson to Sir Thomas Fowell Buxton, 25 September 1833, Clarkson MSS, Henry E. Huntington Library, San Marino, CA; quoted by Morgan, *Slavery and the British Empire*, p.192.

21 It is true that the number of sugar plantations in Jamaica had been declining since the beginning of the century – from 830 in 1804 to 670 in 1834, amounting to a reduction of 19 per cent over 30 years. However, after the abolition of the institution of slavery the decline sharpened markedly, showing a reduction of 51 per cent over 20 years from 1834 to 1854. See Kenneth Morgan, *A Concise History of Jamaica* (Cambridge: Cambridge University Press, 2023), pp 158–9: 'The sugar plantation economy experienced significant decline after slave emancipation. Planters faced increased costs and no longer had access to a permanent, coerced set of workers after apprenticeship ended in 1838. The 670 sugar estates in existence in 1834 fell to 330 in 1854 and 200 in 1880. Failure to prevent plantations incurring serious indebtedness led to the abandonment of 140 sugar properties between 1832 and 1847.'

22 Banner, *Britain's Slavery Debt*, p.24.

23 ibid., pp 30, 54.

24 ibid., p.2.

25 J. Harry Bennett, *Bondsmen and Bishops: Slavery and Apprenticeship on the Codrington Plantations of Barbados, 1710–1838* (Berkeley, CA: University of California Press, 1958), p.10.

26 ibid., p.27.

27 ibid., p.89.

28 ibid., pp 90–91.

29 ibid., pp 124–5.

30 ibid., p.102.

31 ibid., pp 106, 141.

32 ibid., pp 113, 115.

33 ibid., pp 125, 128, 129.

34 ibid., pp 131–3.

35 Morgan, *Slavery and the British Empire*, pp 100–101; Gad Heuman, 'The British West Indies', in Louis (ed.), *The Oxford History of the British Empire*, vol.iii: 'The Nineteenth Century', ed. Andrew Porter.

36 Banner, *Britain's Slavery Debt*, p.35.

37 ibid., p.26.

38 ibid., p.viii.

39 ibid., p.27.

40 There is the hint in what Banner writes that indentured servitude was just another form of slavery. That is not so, as I explained in Chapter 3. Indians, and even some emancipated slaves who had relocated to Sierra Leone, freely signed contracts or 'indentures' that bound them to serve their employer in the West Indies for between one and five years. After a certain period, they would qualify for free passage home. The fact that in British Guiana and Trinidad 'more than two-thirds of the Indians chose to remain rather than return to India' suggests that indentured servitude offered desirable opportunities (Heuman, 'The British West Indies', pp 484–5).

41 Banner, *Britain's Slavery Debt*, p.29.

42 ibid., p.27; quoting B.W. Higman, *A Concise History of the Caribbean*, 2nd edn (Cambridge: Cambridge University Press, 2021), p.205.

7 CONTEXT 4: BRITISH ANTI-SLAVERY

1 Foreign and Commonwealth Office, *Slavery in Diplomacy: The Foreign Office and the Suppression of the Transatlantic Slave Trade*, History Notes, no.17 (London: Foreign and Commonwealth Office, 2007): https://issuu.com/fcohistorians/docs/history_notes_cover_hphn_17 (accessed 4 April 2025), ch.2, esp. pp v, 29, 46.

2 Cited by Andrew Porter, 'Trusteeship, Anti-Slavery, and Humanitarianism', in Louis (ed.), *The Oxford History of the British Empire*, vol.iii, ed. Porter, p.211.

3 David Eltis, *Economic Growth and the Ending of the Transatlantic Slave Trade* (Oxford: Oxford University Press, 1987), pp 92–3, table 2.

4   Leslie Bethell, *The Abolition of the Brazilian Slave Trade: Britain, Brazil and the Slave Trade Question, 1807–1869* (Cambridge: Cambridge University Press, 1979), p.360.

5   Thomas Fowell Buxton, *The African Slave Trade and Its Remedy* (London: John Murray, 1839).

6   Michael W. Doyle, *Empires* (Ithaca, NY: Cornell University Press, 1986), pp 181, 185.

7   Basil S. Cave, 'The End of Slavery in Zanzibar and British East Africa', *Journal of the Royal African Society*, 9/33 (October 1909), pp 20–33. Cave served as a British consul in British East Africa and Zanzibar, at rising grades, from 1891 to 1909. John Lonsdale appears to imply that, since the abolition of the legal status of slavery still left the freed slaves economically dependent on Arab landlords, it was of little account: 'East Africa', in Louis (ed.), *The Oxford History of the British Empire*, vol.iv: 'The Twentieth Century', eds Judith M. Brown and W. Roger Louis, p.533. That would be so, however, only if the granting of legal rights against maltreatment counted for nothing.

8   Nancy Gardner Cassels, *Social Legislation of the East India Company: Public Justice versus Public Instruction* (New Delhi: SAGE Publications India, 2010), p.173.

9   Indian Penal Code (1860), sections 367, 370, 371.

10 Victoria Glendinning, *Raffles and the Golden Opportunity, 1781–1826* (London: Profile Books, 2012), pp xv, 45, 121, 198–9.

11 One of the themes of Jeremy Black's *Slavery* is the relative military weakness of European powers in Africa. The assumption of 'African vulnerability', he writes 'is misplaced, indeed woefully so' (p.253). Lest there be any misunderstanding, of the three cases of British military defeat that I mention here, only the last had anything to do with the suppression of slavery.

12 Cave, 'The End of Slavery in Zanzibar and British East Africa', p.22.

13 ibid., p.32.

14 Evelyn Baring, Earl of Cromer, *Modern Egypt*, 2 vols (London: MacMillan, 1908), vol.ii, pp 495, 496–7, 499–500.

15 For an explanation of the method by which these figures were arrived at, see Biggar, *Colonialism*, pp 390–91n.63. Since I first published the figures and explained the method in *Colonialism* in February 2023, no one, to my knowledge, has challenged them.

16 Eltis, *Economic Growth*, pp 96, 97.

17 Chaim D. Kaufmann and Robert A. Pape, 'Explaining Costly International Moral Action: Britain's Sixty-Year Campaign against the Atlantic Slave Trade', *International Organization*, 53/4 (Autumn 1999), pp 634–7, esp. p.636.

18 ibid., p.631.

8 THE POST-COLONIAL CARIBBEAN

1 Banner, *Britain's Slavery Debt*, p.31.

2 ibid., p.2.

3 ibid., pp 2, 32, 33. It seems that the British are to be damned if they don't and damned if they do. Here, Beckles and Banner complain that the British did not industrialise the West Indies. Yet, shortly after, Banner blames industrialisation in Britain for global warming that now threatens low-lying Caribbean islands (ibid., pp 36, 96).

4 ibid., pp 103–4; CARICOM Reparations Commission, 'Ten-Point Reparation Plan': https://caricomreparations.org/caricom/caricoms-10-point-reparation-plan/ (accessed 4 April 2025).

5 Banner, *Britain's Slavery Debt*, pp 34, 36.

6 See Biggar, *Colonialism*, pp 40, 119–20, 254–5, 436n.45, 439–40n.81, 440–41n.84, 475n.180.

7 D.K. Fieldhouse, *The West and the Third World* (Oxford: Blackwell, 1999), p.168; Rudolf von Albertini with Albert Wirz, *European Colonial Rule, 1880–1940: The Impact of the West on India, Southeast Asia, and Africa*, trans. John G. Williamson (Oxford: Clio, 1982), p.507.

8 Philip Brien and Matthew Keep, *The Public Finances: An Historical Overview*, Briefing Paper 8265 (London: House of Commons Library, 20 March 2018): https://researchbriefings.files.parliament.uk/documents/CBP-8265/CBP-8265.pdf (accessed 22 July 2024), p.4; Kenneth Whyte, *Hoover: An Extraordinary Life in Extraordinary Times* (New York: Vintage, 2017), pp 259–60.

9 International Monetary Fund, *Government Expenditure, Percent of GDP* (New York: IMF, 2024): https://www.imf.org/external/datamapper/exp@FPP/USA/FRA/JPN/GBR/SWE/ESP/ITA/ZAF/IND (accessed 22 July 2024).

10 Niall Ferguson, 'British Imperialism Revised: The Costs and Benefits

of "Anglobalization"', Development Research Institute Working Paper Series, no.2, April 2003 (New York: New York University, 2003), pp 12–13; P.J. Cain and A.G. Hopkins, *British Imperialism, 1688–2015*, 3rd edn (London: Routledge, 2016), p.474; P.J. Cain, 'Economics and Empire: The Metropolitan Context', in Louis (ed.), *The Oxford History of the British Empire*, vol.iii, ed. Porter, p.48, table 2.6.

11 A.R. Dilley, 'The Economics of Empire', in Sarah Stockwell (ed.), *The British Empire: Themes and Perspectives* (Oxford: Blackwell, 2008), p.103, referring to Cain, 'Economics and Empire', p.48, table 2.6.

12 Fieldhouse, *The West and the Third World*, p.84; Gareth Austin, 'Economics of Colonialism in Africa', in Célestin Monga and Justin Yifu (eds), *The Oxford Handbook of Africa and Economics*, 2 vols (Oxford: Oxford University Press, 2015), vol.i: 'Context and Concepts', p.528.

13 Fieldhouse, *The West and the Third World*, p.94.

14 Howard Johnson, 'The British Caribbean from Demobilization to Constitutional Decolonization', in Louis (ed.), *The Oxford History of the British Empire*, vol.iv, eds Brown and Louis, p.608.

15 ibid., p.611.

16 ibid., p.612.

17 Heuman, 'The British West Indies', p.487.

18 Johnson, 'The British Caribbean', p.601.

19 Leigh Gardner and Tirthankar Roy, *The Economic History of Colonialism* (Bristol: Bristol University Press, 2020).

20 In personal correspondence with the author on 10 July 2024. Reprinted here with Professor Roy's permission.

21 Personal correspondence.

22 DeLisle Worrell, *Development and Stabilization in Small Open Economies: Theories and Evidence from Caribbean Experience* (Abingdon: Routledge, 2023), p.8.

23 ibid.

24 Banner, *Britain's Slavery Debt*, p.34.

25 World Health Organization: https://www.who.int/countries/brb/ and https://www.who.int/countries/nga/ (accessed 20 February 2025).

26 World Population Review: https://worldpopulationreview.com/country-rankings/literacy-rate-by-country (accessed 20 February 2025).

27 World Bank: https://data.worldbank.org/indicator/NY.GNP.PCAP.CD (accessed 20 February 2025).

28 Patterson, 'Why Has Jamaica Trailed Barbados', p.96.

29 ibid., p.32.

30 ibid., p.103. For example, the Social Partnership System (pp 84ff).

31 'Political ethos' is my rendering of what Patterson calls 'procedural knowledge' (ibid., p.25). What he means in fact is not just a cognitive understanding of proper procedures, but rather a moral absorption of values and norms. So, while he writes of Barbados's colonial inheritance including 'the procedural *knowledge* of how to play the institutional game', he elaborates in terms of 'deeply instituted formal and informal *norms*' and 'European *values*' (ibid., p.107; the emphases are mine).

32 ibid., p.37.

33 ibid., p.54.

34 ibid., p.56.

35 ibid.

36 ibid., pp 61–2, 80.

37 ibid., p.63.

38 ibid., p.110. Patterson does not himself say that this was a fortunate outcome, but he does imply it, in that the adoption of capitalist norms is one of the reasons that Barbados has flourished economically.

39 ibid., p.32. Patterson implies here an endorsement of Henry's view that it was the socialist policies of Manley's government that held Jamaica back economically.

40 ibid., pp 65–7.

41 ibid., pp 69–70.

42 ibid., pp 75–6.

43 ibid., p.110.

44 ibid., p.104.

45 ibid., pp 34–5.

46 ibid., p.83.

47 See, for example, Bazelon et al., *Quantification of Reparations*, pp 8, 37, 38, 39, 47, 76.

48 Shari Renée Hicks, *A Critical Analysis of Post-Traumatic Slave Syndrome: A Multigenerational Legacy of Slavery* (San Francisco, CA: California Institute of Integral Studies, 2015), p.207.

49 Didier Fassin and Richard Rechtman, *The Empire of Trauma: An Inquiry into the Condition of Victimhood*, trans. Rachel Gomme (Princeton, NJ:

Princeton University Press, 2009), p.281. Fassin and Rechtman go so far as to suggest that 'trauma' is more a construct useful for the promotion of financial and political causes than it is a psychological reality: the social prominence of trauma 'may owe less to advances in knowledge than to changes in the moral climate' (p.23); 'we believe that the truth of trauma lies not in the psyche, the mind, or the brain, but in the moral economy of contemporary societies' (p.276). They quote, without demur, the view of the British psychiatrist Derek Summerfield that trauma is a construct developed to promote the right to compensation, which now supports the careers of lawyers, experts, clinicians and therapists in the 'trauma industry' (p.26). Of the 'metaphorical trace' invoked in the demands for reparation by the descendants of slaves and indigenous peoples, they write: 'We would be tempted to call it an ineffable trace, since this memory is as insistently present as its imprint is fleeting, if there were not some researchers in biomedicine who are now claiming that it has a material reality inscribed in neuronal connections and regions of the brain' (p.276). Such a claim is controversial and by no means generally accepted by relevant experts. But even if it were true, it would not demonstrate how far the physical trace left by historic injury – as distinct from other environmental and cultural factors – determines the present state of the original victim's descendants. For a critique of claims of intergenerational trauma in another case – among indigenous Canadians who attended Indian Residential Schools – see Tom Flanagan, 'Reparations for Historical Injustice and Intergenerational Trauma', *Kulturní Studia*, 2 (2022).

9 NAKED EMPEROR I: HILARY BECKLES

1   CARICOM Reparations Commission: https://caricomreparations. org/ (accessed 4 April 2025).

2   For example, in ch.9 alone of Berg and Hudson, *Slavery*, pp 191n.15, 197n.48, 200n.65, 201n.72, 204n.89, 205n.91, 206n.96; and in Banner, *Britain's Slavery Debt*, pp xix, 27–8, 33–4, 153.

3   Banner, *Britain's Slavery Debt*, p.xix.

4   Beckles, *Britain's Black Debt*.

5   ibid., p.xvii.

6   ibid., p.2.

7   ibid., pp 3, 12.
8   Ferguson, *Empire*; Bernard Porter, *British Imperial. What the Empire Wasn't* (London: I.B. Taurus, 2016); Biggar, *Colonialism*. Ferguson leans to the right politically, Porter to the left. Biggar thought he stood in the centre, until the left pushed him to the right.
9   Beckles, *Britain's Black Debt*, p.18.
10 ibid., p.168.
11 ibid., pp 181–2.
12 In private correspondence during 2–5 December 2020, I raised Beckles's claim that most African chiefs opposed the slave trade, and that those who collaborated did so under duress, with Professor Kenneth Morgan, an economic and social historian of the transatlantic slave trade. Morgan commented, 'I have never seen any African historian support such a view'. He also observed that the authority that Beckles cites on the issue, Hugh Thomas, 'was not a slave-trade historian or an Africanist'.
13 Beckles, *Britain's Black Debt*, p.168.
14 ibid., p.23; see also pp 82, 84.
15 ibid., p.xiv.
16 ibid., p.101.
17 ibid., p.4.
18 Blackburn, *The Making of New World Slavery*. Blackburn is Emeritus Professor in the Department of Sociology at the University of Essex.
19 Beckles, *Britain's Black Debt*, pp 101–2.
20 ibid., p.105; quoting David Richardson, 'The Slave Trade, Sugar, and British Economic Growth, 1748–1776', in Barbara L. Solow and Stanley L. Engerman (eds), *British Capitalism and Caribbean Slavery: The Legacy of Eric Williams* (Cambridge: Cambridge University Press, 1987), p.132.
21 Beckles, *Britain's Black Debt*, p.106.
22 Davis, 'Foreword', p.xiv. While David Richardson reported in 2022 that 'some' continue to advocate Williams's thesis that slavery was a major cause of British industrialisation, in the accompanying endnote he cites only one, quarter-of-a-century-old work – Blackburn's 1997 *The Making of New World Slavery*: Richardson, *Principles and Agents: The British Slave Trade and Its Abolition* (Newhaven, CT: Yale University Press, 2022), pp 10, 274.

23 See Biggar, *Colonialism*, ch.6.

24 See above, ch.8, pp 87–8.

25 Williams, *Capitalism and Slavery*, p.105.

26 Richardson, 'The Slave Trade, Sugar, and British Economic Growth', p.132.

27 Morgan, *Slavery and the British Empire*, p.83.

10 NAKED EMPEROR II: THE BRATTLE REPORT

1 Bazelon et al., *Quantification of Reparations*, p.4.

2 Patrick Robinson, 'Introduction to the Report on Reparations for Transatlantic Chattel Slavery in the Americas and the Caribbean', 8 June 2023: https://www.brattle.com/wp-content/uploads/2023/07/Report-on-Reparations-for-Transatlantic-Chattel-Slavery-in-the-Americas-and-the-Caribbean.pdf (accessed 27 March 2025).

3 Bazelon et al., *Quantification of Reparations*.

4 Robinson, 'Introduction', pp 13–14.

5 As David Eltis explained to me in email correspondence of 27 March and 5 May 2025.

6 Bazelon et al., *Quantification of Reparations*, p.47.

7 Robinson, 'Introduction', pp 1–2. The conclusion that Robinson reports was based on four conference papers. The first, mainly treating African law, was by Nora Wittmann, PhD, who describes herself on Amazon as 'an international lawyer, writer and fashion designer' and is the author of *Slavery Reparations Time Is Now: Exposing Lies, Claiming Justice for Global Survival – An International Legal Assessment* (Power of the Trinity Publishers, 2013), which appears to have been self-published. Wittmann makes the claim that African slavery involved none of the barbarities of its European chattel counterpart, that in Africa slaves were accorded rights such as the right to life, and that '[a]ll of the available evidence suggests that, especially in the first decades and centuries, African rulers actively resisted slavery': 'Examining (Il)Legality of Transatlantic Chattel Slavery: African Law', pp 33–4. Not one of these claims squares with the scholarship reported in Chapter 5 of this book. Further, Africa is a very big place containing many, many peoples over tens of thousands of years, yet Wittmann gives no evidence of

having done the comprehensive research necessary to ground her sweeping generalisations. Consequently, she fails to establish that chattel slavery was unlawful across the whole of Africa.

Moving on to European law, Wittmann notes that slavery was much discussed in early modern Europe – for example, by fathers of international law such as Francisco Suarez and Francisco de Vitoria – and that 'none . . . deemed it legal without any restrictions'. From this she moves swiftly to the conclusion that '[t]he evidence is unambiguous that the conducts that were constituted [*sic*] of transatlantic enslavement and slavery were illegal by general principles of law recognized by civilized nations' (ibid., p.38). Nonsense: the ideas of eminent theologians about what the law should be hardly amount to what it actually was.

Mamadou Hébié, Associate Professor of International Law at the Grotius Centre for International Legal Studies at Leiden, does not quite agree with Wittmann. 'If you take the case of forced labor and the transfer of slaves to the Americas', he writes, 'you have enough practice there, which may tend to suggest that at least those colonial powers, those slave trade companies and countries that were participating in slave trade did not see any strong legal difficulty against their business': 'Examining (Il)Legality of Transatlantic Chattel Slavery: International Law, 1450–1550', in Stefanelli and Lovall (eds), *Reparations*, p.40. Nonetheless, he wants to argue that the 'capture' element of chattel slavery – as distinct from the forced labour and transfer elements – was unlawful at the time. This was because the conformity of Aristotle's doctrine of natural slavery with canon law 'was not obvious'; and because just war doctrine only permitted enslavement to exact reparation and deter future attack (ibid., pp 41–2). Yet, controversy over Aristotle and the implications of just war doctrine are not enough to determine international law.

The author of the third paper, Parvathi Menon, was then a doctoral student and adjunct lecturer at the University of Helsinki. Far from asserting the international unlawfulness of chattel slavery in the period 1500–1800, she merely argues that its lawfulness was a matter of controversy and that there was a lot of legal inconsistency: 'Examining (Il)Legality of Transatlantic Chattel Slavery under International Law: 1500–1815', in Stefanelli and Lovall (eds), *Reparations*, pp 55–8.

The paper treating European law in the second decade of the 1800s was written by Michel Erpelding, PhD, who was then associated with the Max Planck Institute in Luxembourg for International, European, and Regulatory Procedural Law. On the one hand – unnerved, I suspect, by the assertions of Wittmann and Hébié – he says that transatlantic chattel slavery was 'largely never legal . . . under universal international law'. But then, on the other hand, he states the opposite:

> The Declaration of the Eight Courts Relative to the Universal Abolition of the Slave Trade signed by eight major Western powers at the Congress of Vienna on February 8, 1815, was *unquestionably a watershed* in international law. For several centuries, Western international law had served as a crucial tool in supporting this practice of transatlantic chattel slavery, either by organizing the trade or by enforcing and protecting the rights of slave holders in the colonies. *Breaking with the centuries of practice, the Vienna Declaration proclaimed the universal and definitive abolition of the trading in Africans as slaves as the common binding goal of all civilized nations.*

'Examining (Il)Legality of Transatlantic Chattel Slavery under International Law: 1815–88', in Stefanelli and Lovall (eds), *Reparations*, pp 59–60; the emphases are mine.
8   Robinson, 'Introduction', p.6.
9   ibid., p.7.
10 Bazelon et al., *Quantification of Reparations*, p.5.
11 Robinson, 'Introduction', p.10.
12 ibid., p.11.
13 Bazelon et al., *Quantification of Reparations*, pp 1, 74.
14 ibid., pp 7, 49, 53.

11 MAKING AMENDS FOR HISTORIC WRONGS
1   See Biggar, *Colonialism*, pp 185–9.
2   Onora O'Neill, 'Rights to Compensation', in *Justice across Boundaries: Whose Obligations?* (Cambridge: Cambridge University Press, 2016), p.51.

3   Eric A. Posner and Adrian Vermeule analyse the difficulty of 'netting
    out' the benefits and costs of the wrong of slavery: slaves benefited
    from European enslavement insofar as the alternative was slaughter
    back home by an enemy; many wrongdoers passed their unjust profits
    to descendants who made sacrifices for the sake of slaves; some
    descendants of slaves are also the descendants of slave-masters and
    would not exist but for slavery: 'Reparations for Slavery and Other
    Historical Injustices', *Columbia Law Review*, 103/689 (2003), pp 702,
    708, 740. Mark Milke summarises the general problem eloquently:

> At some point, too many waves really have crashed onto the shore
> of our collective histories and retreated, and any effect from deeds
> committed long ago removed with the receding tide ... Beyond
> clear lines of theft to thief, slaveholder to slave, or murderer to
> those who perished, entire countries and their populations alive
> today would be caught in impossible calculations if the working
> assumption for justice is that an act from the distant past can be
> partly remedied with compensation today, or even that it should
> serve as the basis for active discrimination between groups today
> ... the further one travels down historical paths long overgrown by
> the thickets of newer generations, peoples, immigrants, and other
> possible causes for today's observed effects, the more impossible
> it is to begin, never mind finish, such calculations. Beyond tight
> provable links between harm and harmed in recent generations
> and decades, it is otherwise preferable to avoid the impossible
> calculations that seek cosmic justice from the dead. Let them –
> and us – rest in peace.

*The Victim Cult: How the Grievance Culture Hurts Everyone and Wrecks
    Civilizations* (Parksville, BC: Thomas and Black, 2019), pp 237, 246.
4   Richard Vernon, *Historical Redress: Must We Pay for the Past?* (London:
    Continuum, 2012), pp 108–9.
5   John Torpey reports that in the Organisation of African Unity summit
    of 1993, which was convened to consider the African reparations
    campaign, '[t]he role of North Africans and Middle Easterners – not
    to mention sub-Saharan Africans themselves – in the slave trade
    threatened to muddy the historical waters': 'Making Whole What

Has Been Smashed: Reflections on Reparations', *Journal of Modern History*, 73/2 (June 2001), p.353.

6   Unfortunately, I have been unable to retrieve my copy of the letter and identify the date of its publication. The same point was made memorably in an episode of the incomparable television series *The West Wing*, where Josh Lyman, the White House's Deputy Chief of Staff, is talking to Jeff Breckenridge, an African American lawyer who is pressing the case for reparations for slavery. Says Lyman: 'You know, Jeff, I'd love to give you the money. I really would. But I'm a little short of cash right now. It seems the SS officer forgot to give my grandfather his wallet back when he let him out of Birkenau.' See Torpey, 'Making Whole What Has Been Smashed', p.356.

7   Jeremy Waldron, 'Superseding Historic Injustice', *Ethics*, 103/1 (October 1992), p.27.

8   O'Neill, 'Rights to Compensation', p.52; the emphases are O'Neill's. The political philosopher David Miller concurs. Miller writes, 'Thus we might think that colonial nations have special remedial responsibilities to their impoverished former colonies without delving into contested questions such as whether colonialism unjustly enriched the metropolis at the expense of the periphery': *National Responsibility and Global Justice* (Oxford: Oxford University Press, 2007), pp 139–40.

9   Alan C. Cairns, *Citizens Plus: Aboriginal Peoples and the Canadian State* (Vancouver: UBC Press, 2000), p.52.

12 THE CHURCH OF ENGLAND'S RUSH TO REPENTANCE

1   There is some uncertainty about what exactly the Church Commissioners have committed themselves – and the Church – to. An abbreviation of a longer report presented to the Commissioners in November 2023 was published as *Oversight Group Recommendations* in March 2024. The report's recommendations were 'warmly welcomed' by the Board of Governors of the Church Commissioners. A press release stated that the 'Church of England's investment arm accepts the report in full': 'Church Commissioners for England Warmly Welcomes Oversight Group's Report', 4 March 2024: https://www.churchofengland.org/media/press-releases/church-commissioners-england-warmly-welcomes-oversight-groups-report (accessed 4

April 2025). And an editor's note in the report itself explains that 'while these recommendations are couched in conditional language, the Church Commissioners have already agreed to adopt them': *Oversight Group Recommendations to the Board of Governors: Healing, Repair, and Justice* (London: Church Commissioners for England, 2024): https://www.churchofengland.org/sites/default/files/2024-03/ church-commissioners-for-england-oversight-group-report-to-the-board-of-governors.pdf (accessed 4 April 2025), p.2. Yet, there are two discrepancies.

First, the Church Commissioners do not in fact intend simply to 'disburse' £100 million, as claimed on page 2 of the *Oversight Group Recommendations*. They intend to deploy £100 million to create an 'in-perpetuity impact endowment investment fund . . . that will grow over time': 'The Church Commissioners for England: Historic Links to African Chattel Enslavement. Frequently Asked Questions', no date: https://www.churchofengland.org/sites/default/files/2024-06/ the-church-commissioners-for-england-links-to-african-chattel-enslavement-frequently-asked-questions.pdf (accessed 4 April 2025), p.1. If it is to grow, the fund cannot all be spent down. This implies that only a portion of its capital and annual profits will be disbursed. Indeed, the *Oversight Group Recommendations* mentions £30 million (recommendation 11, p.9).

Second, it is unclear whether the fund will build up over five or nine years. As the 'Frequently Asked Questions' document published by the Church Commissioners says, confusingly, 'The Oversight Group have recommended accelerating the rate of investment so that £100 million is deployed in a five-year period. We will continue to honour our funding commitments to the Church while exploring how best to accelerate the deployment of the £100m, which will still span three triennia funding periods' (p.7).

2   Church Commissioners for England, 'Church Commissioners' Links to African Chattel Enslavement': https://www.churchofengland.org/ historic-links-to-enslavement (accessed 4 April 2025).

3   Church Commissioners for England, *Church Commissioners' Research into Historic Links to Transatlantic Chattel Slavery* (London: Church Commissioners for England, 2023): https:// www.churchofengland.org/sites/default/files/2023-01/

church-commissioners-for-england-research-into-historic-links-to-transatlantic-chattel-slavery-report.pdf (accessed 4 April 2025), p.7.

4 Church Commissioners, *Oversight Group Recommendations*, p.5.

5 ibid., p.2.

6 ibid., p.5.

7 ibid., p.3.

8 Church Commissioners, 'Frequently Asked Questions', pp 1–2.

9 ibid., pp 1, 7.

10 At least one member of the Oversight Group, Richard Drayton, Professor of Imperial History at King's College, London, must have known this – and yet he allowed the group's report to overlook it. Scrupulous carefulness, however, is not Professor Drayton's forte. See Nigel Biggar, 'The Drayton Icon and Intellectual Vice', *Quillette*, 27 August 2019: https://quillette.com/2019/08/27/the-drayton-icon-and-intellectual-vice/ (accessed 6 June 2025).

11 Goldman and Tombs, 'The Church of England's Historic Links'.

12 ibid.

13 Richard Dale, 'Slavery Did Dot Benefit Bounty', *Church Times*, 22 March 2024: https://www.churchtimes.co.uk/articles/2024/22-march/comment/opinion/slavery-did-not-benefit-bounty (accessed 4 April 2025).

14 Richard Dale, *The First Crash: Lessons from the South Sea Bubble* (Princeton, NJ: Princeton University Press, 2004).

15 Dale, 'Slavery Did Not Benefit Bounty'.

16 Church Commissioners, *Research into Historic Links*, p.8.

17 Dale, 'Slavery Did Not Benefit Bounty'.

18 Goldman and Tombs, 'The Church of England's Historic Links'.

19 François Velde, 'An Institutional Investor in Eighteenth Century Britain', Federal Reserve Bank of Chicago Working Paper (Chicago, IL: Federal Reserve Bank of Chicago, 2025), p.17. This was originally delivered at the University of Cambridge on 28 May 2024.

20 Church Commissioners, *Research into Historic Links*, p.8.

21 ibid., p.36.

22 ibid., p.26.

23 ibid., p.35.

24 Kenneth Morgan, *Edward Colston and Bristol*, Bristol Historical Association Pamphlets no.96 (Bristol: BHA, 1999): https://archive.

org/details/bha096/page/n3/mode/2up (accessed 3 May 2025), p.2.

25 Kenneth Morgan, 'Colston, Edward', *Oxford Dictionary of National Biography* (Oxford: Oxford University Press, 2004): https://www.oxforddnb.com/ (accessed 5 May 2025).

26 Church Commissioners, *Research into Historic Links*, p.7; Church Commissioners, *Oversight Group Recommendations*, p.5.

27 Church Commissioners, *Oversight Group Recommendations*, p.3.

28 Goldman and Tombs first alerted me to this in 'The Church of England's Historic Links': 'The report's interpretation of the sources seems based on the idea that money would be morally tainted by any degree of association with slavery and the slave trade, carrying that moral stain through the generations to the present day even when the original funds and assets are long gone'.

29 Justin Welby, Archbishop of Canterbury, 'Archbishop's Sermon at a Special Reconciliation Service in Zanzibar', 12 May 2024: https://www.archbishopofcanterbury.org/news/news-and-statements/archbishops-sermon-special-reconciliation-service-zanzibar (accessed 3 May 2025).

30 Alexander Chula, 'In Search of Forgotten Heroes: The Church Has Consigned to Oblivion Those Who Risked All to End the Slave Trade', *The Critic*, 28 November 2024: https://thecritic.co.uk/issues/december-january-2025/in-search-of-forgotten-heroes/ (accessed 3 May 2025).

31 Tim Jeal, *Livingstone*, rev. edn (New Haven, CT, and London: Yale University Press, 2013), p.354.

32 Both the Archbishops of Canterbury and of York have spoken as if the sin of enslavement is one of which the present Church of England is guilty, and as if the Church, along with the rest of the country, had not repented in 1807 and 1833 and spent the following century and a half doing penance. Thus, Archbishop Justin Welby is said to have 'apologised' and has declared that the Church of England's involvement in chattel enslavement is to its 'eternal shame': Church Commissioners, 'Frequently Asked Questions', p.3. And Archbishop Stephen Cottrell has written that 'we must all be responsible for our sins': Church Commissioners for England, *Speeches Delivered to General Synod* (London: Church Commissioners, February 2024), p.1.

33 Church Commissioners for England, 'Church Commissioners

Announce Members of Oversight Group to Advise on Response to Historic Links to Transatlantic Slavery', 24 July 2023: https://www.churchofengland.org/media/press-releases/church-commissioners-announce-members-oversight-group-advise-response-historic (accessed 4 April 2025).

34 Indeed, it is arguable that the Commissioners were delinquent in discharging their duties as trustees. According to guidance published by the UK's Charity Commission, 'constructive debate and challenge are signs of healthy governance': 'Decision-Making for Charity Trustees', 9 September 2024: https://www.gov.uk/government/publications/its-your-decision-charity-trustees-and-decision-making/decision-making-for-charity-trustees (accessed 23 March 2025). Accordingly, trustees should 'critically and objectively review proposals and challenge assumptions in making decisions . . . Trustees who simply defer to the opinions and decisions of others aren't fulfilling their duties': 'The Essential Trustee: What You Need to Know, What You Need to Do', 3 May 2018: https://www.gov.uk/government/publications/the-essential-trustee-what-you-need-to-know-cc3/ (accessed 23 March 2025).

14 CONCLUSION: SO, WHY THE LUST FOR SELF-CONDEMNATION?

1 Bruce Pascoe, *Dark Emu. Black Seeds: Agriculture or Accident?* (Broome, WA: Magabala Books, 2014).

2 Peter O'Brien, *Bitter Harvest: The Illusion of Aboriginal Agriculture in Bruce Pascoe's Dark Emu* (Balmain, NSW: Quadrant Books, 2019).

3 Peter Sutton and Keryn Walshe, *Farmers or Hunter Gatherers: The Dark Emu Debate* (Carlton, VIC: Melbourne University Publishing, 2021).

4 See the Melbourne University Publishing website: https://www.mup.com.au/books/farmers-or-hunter-gatherers-paperback-softback (accessed 1 April 2025).

5 Mary Ellen Turpel-Lafond, 'The Discovery of a Mass Gravesite at a Former Residential School at Kamloops Is Just the Tip of the Iceberg', *Globe and Mail*, 30 May 2021: https://www.theglobeandmail.com/opinion/article-the-discovery-of-a-mass-grave-at-a-former-residential-school-is-just/ (accessed 31 March 2025).

6 Nina Green, 'Why Was a Century-Old Septic Field Installed to Dispose of the Kamloops Indian Residential School's Sewage

Mistaken for "the Remains of 215 Children"?', *Woke Watch Canada*, 28 March 2025: https://wokewatchcanada.substack.com/p/why-was-a-century-old-septic-field (accessed 4 April 2025).

7 J.R. Miller, *Shingwauk's Vision: A History of Native Residential Schools* (Buffalo, NY: University of Toronto Press, 1996), p.142.

8 Greg Piasetzki, '"Genocide"? Canada's Government Wanted to Close Every Indian Residential School in the 1940s', *C2C Journal*, 26 February 2024: https://c2cjournal.ca/2024/02/genocide-canadas-government-wanted-to-close-every-indian-residential-school-in-the-1940s/ (accessed 4 April 2025).

9 ibid.

10 Truth and Reconciliation Commission of Canada, *Final Report*, 5 vols (Toronto: Lorimer, 2015), vol.iv, 'Missing Children and Unmarked Burials', p.21, table 4.

11 Greg Piasetzki, 'Everybody's Favourite Dead White Male: The Mysterious Resurrection and Celebration of Dr Peter Henderson Bryce', *C2C Journal*, 12 November 2021: https://c2cjournal.ca/2021/11/everybodys-favourite-dead-white-male-the-mysterious-resurrection-and-celebration-of-dr-peter-henderson-bryce/ (accessed 4 April 2025).

12 National Centre for Truth and Reconciliation, 'Memorial Register': https://nctr.ca/memorial/national-student-memorial/memorial-register/ (accessed 4 April 2025): 'Through this Register, the NCTR honours the children that were lost because of their attendance at residential schools. This includes those children who passed away within one year of being at a residential school and are considered to have remained under the responsibility of residential school authorities'; see also 'Student Memorial Register: FAQ': https://nctr.ca/memorial/national-student-memorial/student-memorial-register-faq/ (accessed 4 April 2025).

13 David Alexander Robertson and Scott B. Henderson, *Betty. The Helen Betty Osborne Story* (Winnipeg: HighWater Press, 2015).

14 Miller, *Shingwauk's Vision*, pp 335, 424: sexual exploitation of pupils by other, usually older and bigger, students was 'distressingly common' and 'the evidence is overwhelming that a great deal of the sexual exploitation and violence perpetrated on male, and in rare instances female, students was the work of older students'.

15 J.S. Milloy, *'Suffer the Little Children': The Aboriginal Residential School*

System, 1830–1992 (Ottawa: Royal Commission on Aboriginal Peoples, 1996): https://publications.gc.ca/collections/collection_2017/bcp-pco/ Z1-1991-1-41-155-eng.pdf (accessed 3 May 2025). Milloy reports that '[t]he Indian Workers Association of the Presbyterian Church for Saskatchewan and Alberta warned that "half grown girls and boys" at day schools "even upon nominally Christian reserves are imbued with immoral ideals regarding sexual relations"' (p.28). While he accuses the 'official files' of obscuring the sexual abuse of children by adults, he nonetheless relays reports that 'focus on the sexual behaviour of the children, on a concern for intercourse among the children – boys sneaking into the girls' dorm or, with greater frequency, reports of homosexual behaviour among the boys' (pp 451–2). For first-hand corroboration of this from a former pupil, see Tomson Highway, *Permanent Astonishment: Growing Up Cree in the Land of Snow and Sky*, Kindle edn (Toronto: Doubleday Canada, 2022), p.278.

16 Rodney A. Clifton and Mark Dewolf, 'Putting the TRC Report into Context', in Rodney A. Clifton and Mark Dewolf, *From Truth Comes Reconciliation: An Assessment of the Truth and Reconciliation Report* (Winnipeg: Frontier Centre for Public Policy, 2021), pp 43–4.

17 Miller, *Shingwauk's Vision*, pp 143, 422.

18 Rod C. Macleod, *The North-West Mounted Police and Law Enforcement, 1873–1905* (Toronto: University of Toronto Press, 1976), p.3.

19 Ged Martin, 'The Department of Indian Affairs in the Dominion of Canada Budget, 1882', *Martinalia*, 2025: https://www.gedmartin.net/ martinalia-mainmenu-3/312-indian-affairs-1882-budget (accessed 4 April 2025).

20 Olivia Stefanovich, 'Bill before Parliament Would Outlaw Residential School "Denialism"', *CBC News*, 26 September 2024: https://www.cbc. ca/news/politics/ndp-mp-private-members-bill-residential-school-denialism-1.7334916 (accessed 1 April 2025).

21 Church Commissioners, *Research into Historic Links*, p.5.

22 Miller, *Shingwauk's Vision*, p.341: 'What is sometimes disturbing is that at last some former pupils with positive memories tried unsuccessfully to place their positive recollections before the public via the press and electronic media, only to be rebuffed or ignored. For the most part, former students and former staff members who wish to provide a positive recollection or introduce some balance into the media

depictions of residential school life have been relegated to the pages of denominational publications.'

23 Church Commissioners, 'Frequently Asked Questions', pp 2, 7.

24 Church Commissioners, *Research into Historic Links*, p.5.

25 Banner, *Britain's Slavery Debt*, p.ix.

26 ibid., p.x.

27 ibid.

28 ibid., p.xi.

29 George Orwell, 'The Lion and the Unicorn: Socialism and the English Genius', in *England Your England. Notes on a Nation* (London: Pushkin Press, 2021), pp 112–13.

30 ibid., p.112.

31 The Gospel of Matthew, 6.5–6: 'And when you pray, do not be like the hypocrites, for they love to pray standing in the synagogues and on the street corners to be seen by others. Truly I tell you, they have received their reward in full. But when you pray, go into your room, close the door and pray to your Father, who is unseen. Then your Father, who sees what is done in secret, will reward you' (New International Version).

32 Pascal Bruckner, *The Tyranny of Guilt: An Essay on Western Masochism*, trans. Steven Rendall (Princeton, NJ: Princeton University Press, 2010), pp. 34–5.

33 ibid., pp 100–101.

34 George Eliot, *Middlemarch: A Study of Provincial Life* (London: David Campbell, 1991), p.889.

BIBLIOGRAPHY

Affonso I. *Correspondence de Dom Affonso, roi du Congo, 1506–43*. Ed. Louis Jadin and Mireille Decorato. Brussels: Académie Royale des Sciences d'Outre Mer, 1974.

Albertini, Rudolf von, with Albert Wirz. *European Colonial Rule, 1880–1940: The Impact of the West on India, Southeast Asia, and Africa*. Trans. John G. Williamson. Oxford: Clio, 1982.

Allen, R.C. 'Why the Industrial Revolution was British: Commerce, Induced Invention, and the Scientific Revolution.' In *The Economic History Review*, 64/2 (May 2011).

Andrews, Kehinde. *The New Age of Empire: How Racism and Colonialism Still Rule the World*. London: Penguin Books, 2022.

Anstey, Roger. 'Capitalism and Slavery: A Critique.' In *The Economic History Review*, new series, 21/2 (August 1968).

—. *The Atlantic Slave Trade and British Abolition, 1760–1810*. London: Macmillan, 1975.

Ashton, T.S. *The Industrial Revolution 1760–1830*. Oxford: Oxford University Press, 1997.

Austin, Gareth. 'Economics of Colonialism in Africa.' In Célestin Monga and Justin Yifu, eds, *The Oxford Handbook of Africa and Economics*. 2 vols. Oxford: Oxford University Press, 2015, vol.i: 'Context and Concepts.'

Banner, Michael. *Britain's Slavery Debt: Reparations Now!* Oxford: Oxford University Press, 2024.

Bazelon, Coleman, Alberto Vargas, Rohan Janakiraman and Mary M. Olson. *Quantification of Reparations for Transatlantic Chattel Slavery*. New York: Brattle Group, 8 June 2023: https://www.brattle. com/wp-content/uploads/2023/07/Report-on-Reparations-for-Transatlantic-Chattel-Slavery-in-the-Americas-and-the-Caribbean.

pdf (accessed 21 March 2025).

Beckles, Hilary M. *Britain's Black Debt: Reparations for Caribbean Slavery and Native Genocide*. Kingston, Jamaica: University of West Indies Press, 2013.

Behrendt, Stephen D. 'The Transatlantic Slave Trade.' In Paquette and Smith, eds, *The Oxford Handbook of Slavery in the Americas*.

—, A.J.H. Latham, and David A. Northrup. *The Diary of Antera Duke, an Eighteenth-Century African Slave Trader*. New York: Oxford University Press, 2010.

Bellaigue, Christopher de. *The Golden Throne: The Curse of a King*. London: Bodley Head, 2025.

Bennett, J. Harry. *Bondsmen and Bishops: Slavery and Apprenticeship on the Codrington Plantations of Barbados, 1710–1838*. Berkeley, CA: University of California Press, 1958.

Berg, Maxine, and Pat Hudson. *Slavery, Capitalism, and the Industrial Revolution*. London: Polity, 2023.

Bethell, Leslie. *The Abolition of the Brazilian Slave Trade: Britain, Brazil and the Slave Trade Question, 1807–1869*. Cambridge: Cambridge University Press, 1979.

Biggar, Nigel. 'The Drayton Icon and Intellectual Vice.' In *Quillette*, 27 August 2019: https://quillette.com/2019/08/27/the-drayton-icon-and-intellectual-vice/ (accessed 6 June 2025).

—. *Colonialism: A Moral Reckoning*. London: William Collins, 2023, 2024.

—. 'Residential Schools Were No "Atrocity". Just Look at the Evidence.' In *National Post*, 2 April 2025: https://nationalpost.com/opinion/nigel-biggar-residential-schools-were-no-atrocity-just-look-at-the-evidence (accessed 11 April 2025).

Binnema, Ted. *The Vancouver Island Treaties and the Evolving Principles of Indigenous Title*. Toronto: University of Toronto, 2025.

Black, Jeremy. *Slavery: A New Global History*. London: Constable and Robinson, 2011.

Blackburn, Robin. *The Making of New World Slavery: From the Baroque to the Modern, 1492–1800*. London: Verso, 1997.

Brien, Philip, and Matthew Keep. *The Public Finances: An Historical Overview*. Briefing Paper 8265. London: House of Commons Library, 20 March 2018: https://researchbriefings.files.parliament.uk/documents/CBP-8265/CBP-8265.pdf (accessed 22 July 2024).

Brown, Jonathan A.C. *Slavery and Islam*. London: Oneworld Academic, 2019.

Bruckner, Pascal. *The Tyranny of Guilt: An Essay on Western Masochism*. Trans. Steven Rendall. Princeton, NJ: Princeton University Press, 2010.

Buxton, Thomas Fowell. *The African Slave Trade and Its Remedy*. London: John Murray, 1839.

Cain, P.J. 'Economics and Empire: The Metropolitan Context.' In Louis, ed., *The Oxford History of the British Empire*, vol.iii: 'The Nineteenth Century', ed. Andrew Porter.

—, and A.G. Hopkins. *British Imperialism, 1688–2015*. 3rd edn. London: Routledge, 2016.

Cairns, Alan C. *Citizens Plus: Aboriginal Peoples and the Canadian State*. Vancouver: UBC Press, 2000.

Campbell, Mavis C. *The Maroons of Jamaica, 1655–1796*. Granby, MA: Bergin and Garvin, 1988.

Caretta, Vincent. *Equiano, the African: Biography of a Self-Made Man*. Athens: University of Georgia Press, 2005.

CARICOM. 'Reparations for Native Genocide and Slavery', 13 October 2015: https://caricom.org/reparations-for-native-genocide-and-slavery/ (accessed 4 April 2025).

CARICOM Reparations Commission. 'Ten-Point Reparation Plan': https://caricomreparations.org/caricom/caricoms-10-point-reparation-plan/ (accessed 4 April 2025).

Carroll, Rory. 'New Book Reopens Old Arguments about Slave Raids on Europe.' In *Guardian*, 11 March 2004: https://www.theguardian.com/uk/2004/mar/11/highereducation.books (accessed 4 April 2025).

Cassels, Nancy Gardner. *Social Legislation of the East India Company: Public Justice versus Public Instruction*. New Delhi: SAGE Publications India, 2010.

Cave, Basil S. 'The End of Slavery in Zanzibar and British East Africa.' In *Journal of the Royal African Society*, 9/33 (October 1909).

Charity Commission. 'The Essential Trustee: What You Need to Know, What You Need to Do', 3 May 2018: https://www.gov.uk/government/publications/the-essential-trustee-what-you-need-to-know-cc3/ (accessed 23 March 2025).

—. 'Decision-Making for Charity Trustees', 9 September 2024: https://

www.gov.uk/government/publications/its-your-decision-charity-trustees-and-decision-making/decision-making-for-charity-trustees (accessed 23 March 2025).

Chula, Alexander. 'In Search of Forgotten Heroes: The Church Has Consigned to Oblivion Those Who Risked All to End the Slave Trade.' In *The Critic*, 28 November 2024: https://thecritic.co.uk/issues/december-january-2025/in-search-of-forgotten-heroes/ (accessed 3 May 2025).

Church Commissioners for England. 'The Church Commissioners for England: Historic Links to African Chattel Enslavement. Frequently Asked Questions', no date: https://www.churchofengland.org/sites/default/files/2024-06/the-church-commissioners-for-england-links-to-african-chattel-enslavement-frequently-asked-questions.pdf (accessed 4 April 2025).

—. 'Church Commissioners' Links to African Chattel Enslavement', no date: https://www.churchofengland.org/historic-links-to-enslavement (accessed 4 April 2025).

—. *Church Commissioners' Research into Historic Links to Transatlantic Chattel Slavery.* London: Church Commissioners for England, 2023: https://www.churchofengland.org/sites/default/files/2023-01/church-commissioners-for-england-research-into-historic-links-to-transatlantic-chattel-slavery-report.pdf (accessed 4 April 2025).

—. 'Church Commissioners Announce Members of Oversight Group to Advise on Response to Historic Links to Transatlantic Slavery', 24 July 2023: https://www.churchofengland.org/media/press-releases/church-commissioners-announce-members-oversight-group-advise-response-historic (accessed 4 April 2025).

—. *Speeches Delivered to General Synod.* London: Church Commissioners, February 2024.

—. 'Church Commissioners for England Warmly Welcomes Oversight Group's Report', 4 March 2024: https://www.churchofengland.org/media/press-releases/church-commissioners-england-warmly-welcomes-oversight-groups-report (accessed 4 April 2025).

—, Oversight Group. *Oversight Group Recommendations to the Board of Governors: Healing, Repair, and Justice.* London: Church Commissioners for England, 2024: https://www.churchofengland.org/sites/default/files/2024-03/

church-commissioners-for-england-oversight-group-report-to-the-board-of-governors.pdf (accessed 4 April 2025).

Clifton, Rodney A., and Mark Dewolf. 'Putting the TRC Report into Context.' In Rodney A. Clifton and Mark Dewolf, *From Truth Comes Reconciliation: An Assessment of the Truth and Reconciliation Report.* Winnipeg: Frontier Centre for Public Policy, 2021.

Commission on Race and Ethnic Disparities (CRED). *The Report.* London: HMSO, 2021: https://assets.publishing.service.gov.uk/media/6062ddb1d3bf7f5ce1060aa4/20210331_-_CRED_Report_-_FINAL_-_Web_Accessible.pdf (accessed 21 March 2025).

Craton, Michael. *Testing the Chains: Resistance to Slavery in the British West Indies.* Ithaca, NY: Cornell University Press, 1982.

Cromer, Evelyn Baring, Earl of. *Modern Egypt.* 2 vols. London: MacMillan, 1908.

Curtin, Philip D. *The Atlantic Slave Trade: A Census.* Madison, WI: University of Wisconsin Press, 1969.

Dale, Richard. *The First Crash: Lessons from the South Sea Bubble.* Princeton, NJ: Princeton University Press, 2004.

—. 'Slavery Did Not Benefit Bounty.' In *Church Times,* 22 March 2024: https://www.churchtimes.co.uk/articles/2024/22-march/comment/opinion/slavery-did-not-benefit-bounty (accessed 4 April 2025).

Davis, David Brion. 'Foreword.' In Seymour Drescher, *Econocide: British Slavery in the Era of Abolition.* 2nd edn. Chapel Hill, NC: University of North Carolina Press, 2010.

Davis, Robert C. *Christian Slaves, Muslim Masters: White Slavery in the Mediterranean, the Barbary Coast and Italy, 1500–1800.* London: Palgrave Macmillan, 2003.

Dilley, A.R. 'The Economics of Empire.' In Sarah Stockwell, ed., *The British Empire: Themes and Perspectives.* Oxford: Blackwell, 2008.

Donald, Leland. *Aboriginal Slavery on the Northwest Coast of North America.* Berkeley and Los Angeles, CA: University of California Press, 1997.

Doyle, Michael W. *Empires.* Ithaca, NY: Cornell University Press, 1986.

Earle, Peter. *Corsairs of Malta and Barbary.* London: Sidgwick and Jackson, 1970.

Eliot, George. *Middlemarch: A Study of Provincial Life.* London: David Campbell, 1991.

Eltis, David. *Economic Growth and the Ending of the Transatlantic Slave Trade.* Oxford: Oxford University Press, 1987.

—. *Atlantic Cataclysm: Rethinking the Atlantic Slave Trade.* Cambridge: Cambridge University Press, 2024.

—, *The Rise of African Slavery in the Americas.* Cambridge: Cambridge University Press, 2000.

—, and David Richardson. *Atlas of the Transatlantic Slave Trade.* New Haven: Yale University Press, 2025.

—, and Stanley L. Engerman. 'The Importance of Slavery and the Slave Trade to Industrializing Britain.' In *Journal of Economic History*, 60/1 (March 2000).

Equiano, Olaudah. *The Interesting Narrative and Other Writings.* Ed. Vincent Carretta. Rev. edn. New York: Penguin, 2003.

Erpelding, Michel. 'Examining (Il)Legality of Transatlantic Chattel Slavery under International Law: 1815–88.' In Stefanelli and Lovall, eds, *Reparations.*

European Union Agency for Fundamental Rights. *Being Black in the EU: Summary of the Second European Union Minorities and Discrimination Survey.* Vienna: EUAFR, 2019: https://fra.europa.eu/sites/default/files/fra_uploads/fra-2019-being-black-in-the-eu-summary_en.pdf (accessed 21 March 2025).

Fage, J.D. 'African Societies and the Atlantic Slave Trade.' In *Past and Present*, cxxv (1989).

Fassin, Didier, and Richard Rechtman. *The Empire of Trauma: An Inquiry into the Condition of Victimhood.* Trans. Rachel Gomme. Princeton, NJ: Princeton University Press, 2009.

Feinstein, C.H. 'Capital Accumulation and the Industrial Revolution.' In Roderick Floud and Donald McCloskey, eds, *The Economic History of Britain since 1700.* 1st edn. 2 vols. Cambridge: Cambridge University Press, 1981.

Ferguson, Niall. 'British Imperialism Revised: The Costs and Benefits of "Anglobalization".' Development Research Institute Working Paper Series, no.2, April 2003. New York: New York University, 2003.

—. *Empire. How Britain Made the Modern World.* London: Allen Lane, 2003.

Fieldhouse, D.K. *The West and the Third World.* Oxford: Blackwell, 1999.

Flanagan, Tom. 'Reparations for Historical Injustice and

Intergenerational Trauma.' In *Kulturní Studia*, 2 (2022).

Foreign and Commonwealth Office. *Slavery in Diplomacy: The Foreign Office and the Suppression of the Transatlantic Slave Trade.* History Notes, no.17. London: Foreign and Commonwealth Office, 2007: https://issuu.com/fcohistorians/docs/history_notes_cover_hphn_17 (accessed 4 April 2025).

Fulton, John D.O. *Slavery and the Scottish Enlightenment.* Stroud: Fonthill Media, 2024.

Gardner, Leigh, and Tirthankar Roy, *The Economic History of Colonialism.* Bristol: Bristol University Press, 2020.

Glendinning, Victoria. *Raffles and the Golden Opportunity, 1781–1826.* London: Profile Books, 2012.

Godwyn, Morgan. *The Negro's & Indians Advocate, Suing for Their Admission into the Church . . .* London, 1680.

Goldman, Lawrence, and Robert Tombs. 'The Church of England's Historic Links to the Translatlantic Slave Trade.' In *History Reclaimed*, 1 July 2024: https://historyreclaimed.co.uk/the-church-of-englands-historic-links-to-the-transatlantic-slave-trade/ (accessed 1 April 2025).

Gopal, Priyamvada. *Insurgent Empire: Anticolonial Resistance and British Dissent.* London: Verso, 2019.

Gragg, Larry. *Englishmen Transplanted: The English Colonization of Barbados, 1627–1660.* Oxford: Oxford University Press, 2003.

Grammont, Henri-David de. *La course, l'esclavage et la redemption à Alger.* Etudes algériennes. Paris, 1885.

Green, Nina. 'Why Was a Century-Old Septic Field Installed to Dispose of the Kamloops Indian Residential School's Sewage Mistaken for "the Remains of 215 Children"?' *Woke Watch Canada*, 28 March 2025: https://wokewatchcanada.substack.com/p/why-was-a-century-old-septic-field (accessed 4 April 2025).

Hall, Suzanne, et al., *Love Thy Neighbour? Public Trust and Acceptance of the People Who Live Alongside Us.* The UK in the World Values Survey. London: Policy Institute at King's College London, April 2023: https://www.kcl.ac.uk/policy-institute/assets/love-thy-neighbour.pdf (accessed 21 March 2025).

Hämäläinen, Pekka. *The Comanche Empire.* New Haven, CT, and London: Yale University Press, 2008.

Handler, Jerome S., and Matthew C. Reilly. 'Contesting "White Slavery" in the Caribbean: Enslaved Africans and European Indentured Servants in Seventeenth-Century Barbados.' In *New West Indian Guide*, 91 (2017).

Hazareesingh, Sudhir. *Black Spartacus: The Epic Life of Toussaint Louverture*. London: Allen Lane, 2020.

Hébié, Mamadou. 'Examining (Il)Legality of Transatlantic Chattel Slavery: International Law, 1450–1550.' In Stefanelli and Lovall, eds, *Reparations*.

Heffer, Greg. 'Labour MPs Demand Britain Pays Reparations to Caribbean Countries for Slave Trade and "400 Years of Hideous Abuse".' In *Mail*, 10 March 2023: https://www.dailymail.co.uk/news/article-11839257/Labour-MPs-demand-Britain-pays-reparations-Caribbean-countries-400-years-hideous-abuse.html (accessed 21 March 2025).

Heuman, Gad. 'The British West Indies.' In Louis, ed., *The Oxford History of the British Empire*, vol.iii: 'The Nineteenth Century', ed. Andrew Porter.

—. 'Slavery, the Slave Trade, and Abolition.' In Louis, ed., *The Oxford History of the British Empire*, vol.v: 'Historiography', ed. Robin Winks.

Heywood, Linda M. 'Slavery and its Transformation in the Kingdom of Kongo, 1491–1800.' In *Journal of African History*, 50/1 (2009).

Hicks, Shari Renée. *A Critical Analysis of Post-Traumatic Slave Syndrome: A Multigenerational Legacy of Slavery*. San Francisco, CA: California Institute of Integral Studies, 2015.

Highway, Tomson. *Permanent Astonishment: Growing Up Cree in the Land of Snow and Sky*. Kindle edn. Toronto: Doubleday Canada, 2022.

Higman, B.W. *A Concise History of the Caribbean*. 2nd edn. Cambridge: Cambridge University Press, 2021.

Hilton, Anne. *The Kingdom of Kongo*. Oxford: Oxford University Press, 1985.

Hochschild, Adam. *King Leopold's Ghost: A Story of Greed, Terror, and Heroism in Colonial Africa*. New York: Houghton Mifflin Harcourt Publishing, 2020.

—. *Bury the Chains: The British Struggle to Abolish Slavery*. London: Macmillan, 2005.

Hogendorn, Jan S., and Paul E. Lovejoy. *Slow Death for Slavery. The Course of Abolition in Northern Nigeria, 1897–1936*. Cambridge: Cambridge University Press, 1993.

Iliffe, John. *Africans: The History of a Continent.* 3rd edn. Cambridge: Cambridge University Press, 2017.

Inikori, Joseph E. 'Slavery in Africa and the Transatlantic Slave Trade.' In Alusine Jalloh and Stephen E. Maizlish, eds, *The African Diaspora.* College Station, TX: Texas A&M University Press, 1966.

International Monetary Fund. *Government Expenditure, Percent of GDP.* New York: IMF, 2024: https://www.imf.org/external/datamapper/exp@FPP/USA/FRA/JPN/GBR/SWE/ESP/ITA/ZAF/IND (accessed 22 July 2024).

Iroko, Abiola Félix. 'Historian: "Africans Must Be Condemned for the Slave Trade"', interview with Abiola Félix Iroko on Benin Web TV, *Free West Media*, 28 July 2020: https://freewestmedia.com/2020/07/28/historian-africans-must-be-condemned-for-the-slave-trade/ (accessed 29 June 2021).

Jeal, Tim. *Livingstone.* Rev. edn. New Haven, CT, and London: Yale University Press, 2013.

Johnson, Howard. 'The British Caribbean from Demobilization to Constitutional Decolonization.' In Louis, ed., *The Oxford History of the British Empire*, vol.iv: 'The Twentieth Century', eds Judith M. Brown and W. Roger Louis.

Kaufmann, Chaim D., and Robert A. Pape. 'Explaining Costly International Moral Action: Britain's Sixty-Year Campaign against the Atlantic Slave Trade.' In *International Organization*, 53/4 (Autumn 1999).

Kedourie, Elie. *In the Anglo-Arab Labyrinth: The McMahon-Husayn Correspondence and Its Interpretations, 1914–1939.* 2nd edn. London: Frank Cass, 2000.

Kitson, Frank. *Prince Rupert: Admiral and General-at-Sea.* London: Constable, 1999.

Lalvani, Kartar. *The Making of India: The Untold Story of British Enterprise.* London: Bloomsbury, 2016.

Law, Robin. 'Human Sacrifice in Pre-Colonial Africa.' In *African Affairs*, 84/334 (January 1985).

Le May, G.H. *British Supremacy in South Africa, 1899–1907.* Oxford: Clarendon Press, 1965.

Levtzion, N., and J.F.P. Hopkins, eds. *Corpus of Early Arabic Sources for West African History.* Cambridge: Cambridge University Press, 1981.

Lonsdale, John. 'East Africa.' In Louis, ed., *The Oxford History of the British Empire*, vol.iv: 'The Twentieth Century', eds Judith M. Brown and W. Roger Louis.

Louis, William Roger, ed. *The Oxford History of the British Empire*. 5 vols. Oxford: Oxford University Press, 1999.

Lownie, Rob. 'Survey: UK Is One of the Least Racist Countries in the World.' In *Unherd*, 27 April 2023: https://unherd.com/newsroom/survey-uk-is-one-of-the-least-racist-countries-in-the-world/ (accessed 21 March 2025).

McKee, Helen. 'From Violence to Alliance: Maroons and White Settlers in Jamaica, 1739–1795.' In *Slavery and Abolition*, 39/1 (2018).

Macleod, Rod C. *The North-West Mounted Police and Law Enforcement, 1873–1905*. Toronto: University of Toronto Press, 1976.

Marmon, Shaun. 'Domestic Slavery in the Mamluk Empire: A Preliminary Sketch.' In Shaun Marmon, ed., *Slavery in the Islamic Middle East*. Princeton, NJ: Markus Wiener, 1999.

Marozzi, Justin. *Captives and Companions: A History of Slavery and the Slave Trade in the Islamic World*. London: Penguin, 2025.

Martin, Ged. 'The Department of Indian Affairs in the Dominion of Canada Budget, 1882.' In *Martinalia*, 2025: https://www.gedmartin.net/martinalia-mainmenu-3/312-indian-affairs-1882-budget (accessed 4 April 2025).

Mellor, George R. *British Imperial Trusteeship, 1783–1850*. London: Faber & Faber, 1951.

Menon, Parvathi. 'Examining (Il)Legality of Transatlantic Chattel Slavery under International Law: 1500–1815.' In Stefanelli and Lovall, eds, *Reparations*.

Milke, Mark. *The Victim Cult: How the Grievance Culture Hurts Everyone and Wrecks Civilizations*. Parksville, BC: Thomas and Black, 2019.

Miller, David. *National Responsibility and Global Justice*. Oxford: Oxford University Press, 2007.

Miller, Joseph C. 'A Global History of the Slave Trade.' In *Journal of African History*, 49/2 (2008).

Miller, J.R. *Shingwauk's Vision: A History of Native Residential Schools*. Buffalo, NY: University of Toronto Press, 1996.

Milloy, J.S. *'Suffer the Little Children': The Aboriginal Residential School System, 1830–1992*. Ottawa: Royal Commission on Aboriginal Peoples,

1996: https://publications.gc.ca/collections/collection_2017/bcp-pco/
Z1-1991-1-41-155-eng.pdf (accessed 3 May 2025).

Mokyr, Joel. 'Editor's Introduction: The New Economic History and
the Industrial Revolution.' In Joel Mokyr, ed., *The British Industrial
Revolution: An Economic Perspective.* 2nd edn. London: Routledge, 1999.

—. *The Enlightened Economy: An Economic History of Britain 1700–1850.*
New Haven, CT: Yale University Press, 2012.

Montesquieu, Charles Louis de Secondat, Baron de. *The Complete Works
of M. de Montesquieu.* 4 vols. London: T. Evans, 1777. Vol.i: 'The Spirit
of Laws.'

Morgan, Kenneth. *Edward Colston and Bristol.* Bristol Historical
Association Pamphlets, no.96. Bristol: BHA, 1999: https://archive.org/
details/bha096/page/n3/mode/2up (accessed 3 May 2025).

—. 'Colston, Edward.' In *Oxford Dictionary of National Biography.* Oxford:
Oxford University Press, 2004: https://www.oxforddnb.com/ (accessed
5 May 2025).

—. *Slavery and the British Empire: From Africa to America.* Oxford: Oxford
University Press, 2007.

—. *A Concise History of Jamaica.* Cambridge: Cambridge University Press,
2023.

National Centre for Truth and Reconciliation. 'Memorial Register':
https://nctr.ca/memorial/national-student-memorial/memorial-
register/ (accessed 4 April 2025).

—. 'Student Memorial Register: FAQ': https://nctr.ca/memorial/
national-student-memorial/student-memorial-register-faq/ (accessed
4 April 2025).

National Park Service. 'Andersonville: The Deadly Confederate Prison
Camp': https://www.battlefields.org/learn/articles/andersonville-
prison (accessed 20 February 2025).

Niezen, Ronald. *The Origins of Indigenism: Human Rights and the Politics of
Identity.* Berkeley, CA: University of California Press, 2003.

O'Brien, Denis. Letter. In *Sunday Telegraph*, 9 February 2025.

O'Brien, Peter. *Bitter Harvest: The Illusion of Aboriginal Agriculture in Bruce
Pascoe's Dark Emu.* Balmain, NSW: Quadrant Books, 2019.

O'Neill, Onora. 'Rights to Compensation.' In Onora O'Neill, *Justice across
Boundaries: Whose Obligations?* Cambridge: Cambridge University
Press, 2016.

Orwell, George. 'The Lion and the Unicorn: Socialism and the English Genius.' In *England Your England. Notes on a Nation*. London: Pushkin Press, 2021.

Pachai, Bridglal. 'Indentured Chinese Immigrant Labour on the Witwatersrand Goldfields.' In *India Quarterly*, 21/1 (January–March 1965).

Paquette, Robert L., and Mark M. Smith, eds. *The Oxford Handbook of Slavery in the Americas*. Oxford: Oxford University Press, 2010.

Pascoe, Bruce. *Dark Emu. Black Seeds: Agriculture or Accident?* Broome, WA: Magabala Books, 2014.

Patterson, Orlando. 'Why Has Jamaica Trailed Barbados on the Path to Sustained Growth? The Role of Institutions, Colonialism, and Cultural Appropriation.' In Orlando Patterson, *The Confounding Island: Jamaica and the Postcolonial Predicament*. Cambridge, MA: Belknap Press, 2019.

Pelteret, David. *Slavery in Early Medieval England: From the Reign of Alfred to the Twelfth Century*. Woodbridge: Boydell Press, 1995.

Pétré-Grenouilleau, Olivier. *Les traites négrières: essai d'histoire globale*. Paris: Editions Gallimard, 2004.

Piasetzki, Greg. 'Everybody's Favourite Dead White Male: The Mysterious Resurrection and Celebration of Dr Peter Henderson Bryce.' In *C2C Journal*, 12 November 2021: https://c2cjournal.ca/2021/11/everybodys-favourite-dead-white-male-the-mysterious-resurrection-and-celebration-of-dr-peter-henderson-bryce/ (accessed 4 April 2025).

—. '"Genocide"? Canada's Government Wanted to Close Every Indian Residential School in the 1940s.' In *C2C Journal*, 26 February 2024: https://c2cjournal.ca/2024/02/genocide-canadas-government-wanted-to-close-every-indian-residential-school-in-the-1940s/ (accessed 4 April 2025).

Porter, Andrew. 'Trusteeship, Anti-Slavery, and Humanitarianism.' In Louis, ed., *The Oxford History of the British Empire*, vol.iii: 'The Nineteenth Century', ed. Andrew Porter.

Porter, Bernard. *British Imperial. What the Empire Wasn't*. London: I.B. Taurus, 2016.

Posner, Eric A., and Adrian Vermeule. 'Reparations for Slavery and Other Historical Injustices.' In *Columbia Law Review*, 103/689 (2003).

Pyrah, G.B. *Imperial Policy and South Africa, 1902–10*. Oxford: Clarendon Press, 1955.

Richardson, David. 'The Slave Trade, Sugar, and British Economic Growth.' In Barbara L. Solow and Stanley L. Engerman, eds, *British Capitalism and Caribbean Slavery: The Legacy of Eric Williams*. Cambridge: Cambridge University Press, 1987.

—. 'The British Empire and the Atlantic Slave Trade, 1660–1807.' In Louis, ed., *The Oxford History of the British Empire*, vol.ii: 'The Eighteenth Century', ed. P.J. Marshall.

—. *Principles and Agents: The British Slave Trade and Its Abolition*. Newhaven, CT: Yale University Press, 2022.

Richardson, Peter. 'The Recruiting of Chinese Indentured Labour for the South African Gold Mines, 1903–1908.' In *Journal of African History*, xviii/1 (1977).

Ritchie, David. *Natural Rights: A Criticism of Some Ethical and Political Conceptions*. London: Swan Sonnenschein, 1895.

Robertson, David Alexander, and Scott B. Henderson. *Betty. The Helen Betty Osborne Story*. Winnipeg: HighWater Press, 2015.

Robinson, Patrick. 'Introduction to the Report on Reparations for Transatlantic Chattel Slavery in the Americas and the Caribbean', 8 June 2023: https://www.brattle.com/wp-content/uploads/2023/07/Report-on-Reparations-for-Transatlantic-Chattel-Slavery-in-the-Americas-and-the-Caribbean.pdf (accessed 27 March 2025).

Rodney, Walter. 'African Slavery and Other Forms of Social Oppression on the Upper Guinea Coast in the Context of the Atlantic Slave Trade.' In *Journal of African History*, 7/3 (1966).

Royle, Trevor. *Civil War: The Wars of the Three Kingdoms, 1638–1660*. London: Abacus, 2004.

Salau, Mohammed Bashir. *Sokoto Caliphate: A Historical and Comparative Study*. Rochester Studies in African History and the Diaspora, vol.80. Martlesham: Boydell & Brewer, 2019.

Sanghera, Sathnam. *Empireland: How Imperialism Has Shaped Modern Britain*. London: Penguin Books, 2021.

Simon, Yves R. *The Ethiopian Campaign and French Political Thought*. Ed. Anthony O. Simon. Trans. Robert Royal. Notre Dame: University of Notre Dame, 2009.

Simpson, Craig. 'Caribbean Lobbyists Funded by Telecoms Billionaire Draft "Bespoke" Reparations Plans.' In *Telegraph*, 10 September 2023: https://www.telegraph.co.uk/news/2023/09/10/

caribbean-lobbyists-billionaire-funding-reparations-demand/ (accessed 21 March 2023).

Slave Voyages Project: https://www.slavevoyages.org/assessment/ estimates.

Smith, Adam. *The Theory of Moral Sentiments*. Ed. Dugald Stewart. London: Henry G. Bohn, 1853.

Sosa, Antonio de. *Topography of Algiers: Attempted Escape of Miguel de Cervantes (c.1577)*. In Mario Klarer, ed., *Barbary Captives: An Anthology of Early Modern Slave Memoirs by Europeans in North Africa*. New York: Columbia University Press, 2022.

Stauffer, John. 'Abolition and Antislavery.' In Paquette and Smith, eds, *The Oxford Handbook of Slavery in the Americas*.

Stefanelli, Justine, and Erin Lovall, eds. *Reparations under International Law for Enslavement of African Persons in the Americas and the Caribbean*. Proceedings of the Symposium of 20–21 May 2021, co-sponsored by the American Society of International Law and the Office of the Vice-Chancellor, the University of the West Indies. Washington, DC: American Society of International Law, 2022.

Stefanovich, Olivia. 'Bill before Parliament Would Outlaw Residential School "Denialism".' In *CBC News*, 26 September 2024: https://www.cbc.ca/news/politics/ndp-mp-private-members-bill-residential-school-denialism-1.7334916 (accessed 1 April 2025).

Stirling, Michelle. 'Mark Carney's Disturbing Silence on Residential School Genocide Claims.' In *Western Standard*, 6 May 2023: https://www.westernstandard.news/opinion/stirling-mark-carneys-disturbing-silence-on-residential-school-genocide-claims/article_1407e424-eb88-11ed-87d0-efa1f4364759.html (accessed 11 April 2025).

Stokes, Doug. 'Did Slavery Make Britain Rich?' In *Doug's Newsletter*, 23 October 2022: https://dougstokes.substack.com/p/did-slavery-make-britain-rich#_ftnref16 (accessed 1 April 2025).

Sutton, Peter, and Keryn Walshe. *Farmers or Hunter Gatherers: The Dark Emu Debate*. Carlton, VIC: Melbourne University Publishing, 2021.

Thornton, John. 'African Political Ethics and the Slave Trade.' In Derek R. Peterson, ed., *Abolitionism and Imperialism in Britain, Africa, and the Atlantic*. Athens, OH: University of Athens Press, 2010.

Torpey, John. 'Making Whole What Has Been Smashed: Reflections on Reparations.' In *Journal of Modern History*, 73/2 (June 2001).

Truth and Reconciliation Commission of Canada. *Final Report*. 5 vols. Toronto: Lorimer, 2015. Vol.iv: 'Missing Children and Unmarked Burials.'

Tugendhat, Michael. 'Human Rights in Britain and France from Thomas Becket to the French Revolution.' Inner Temple History Society Lecture, London, 10 October 2022: https://www.innertemple.org.uk/education/education-resources/history-society-lecture-recordings/human-rights-in-britain-and-france/ (accessed 4 April 2025).

Turpel-Lafond, Mary Ellen. 'The Discovery of a Mass Gravesite at a Former Residential School at Kamloops Is Just the Tip of the Iceberg.' In *Globe and Mail*, 30 May 2021: https://www.theglobeandmail.com/opinion/article-the-discovery-of-a-mass-grave-at-a-former-residential-school-is-just/ (accessed 31 March 2025).

United Nations Declaration on the Rights of Indigenous Peoples, 13 September 2007: https://www.ohchr.org/sites/default/files/Documents/Publications/Declaration_indigenous_en.pdf (accessed 21 March 2025).

Vaughan, Alden T. *Roots of American Racism: Essays on the Colonial Experience*. Oxford: Oxford University Press, 1995.

Veinstein, G. 'Soḳullu Meḥmed Pasha.' In P. Bearman, T. Bianquis, C.E. Bosworth, E. van Donzel and W.P. Heinrichs, eds, *Encyclopaedia of Islam*. 2nd edn. Leiden: Brill, 2012.

Velde, François. 'An Institutional Investor in Eighteenth Century Britain.' Federal Reserve Bank of Chicago Working Paper. Chicago, IL: Federal Reserve Bank of Chicago, 2025.

Vernon, Richard. *Historical Redress: Must We Pay for the Past?* London: Continuum, 2012.

Waldron, Jeremy. 'Superseding Historic Injustice.' In *Ethics*, 103/1 (October 1992).

Welby, Justin, Archbishop of Canterbury. 'Archbishop's Sermon at a Special Reconciliation Service in Zanzibar', 12 May 2024: https://www.archbishopofcanterbury.org/news/news-and-statements/archbishops-sermon-special-reconciliation-service-zanzibar (accessed 3 May 2025).

Wesley, John. *Thoughts Upon Slavery*. London and Philadelphia, PA: John Cruckshank, 1774.

Whyte, Kenneth. *Hoover: An Extraordinary Life in Extraordinary Times*. New York: Vintage, 2017.

Williams, Eric. *Capitalism and Slavery.* Chapel Hill, NC: University of North Carolina Press, 1944.

Wittmann, Nora. 'Examining (Il)Legality of Transatlantic Chattel Slavery: African Law.' In Stefanelli and Lovall, eds, *Reparations.*

World Bank. 'GNI Per Capita, Atlas Method (Current us$)': https://data.worldbank.org/indicator/NY.GNP.PCAP.CD (accessed 20 February 2025).

World Health Organization. 'Barbados': https://www.who.int/countries/brb/ (accessed 20 February 2025).

—. 'Nigeria': https://www.who.int/countries/nga/ (accessed 20 February 2025).

World Population Review. 'Literacy Rate by Country': https://worldpopulationreview.com/country-rankings/literacy-rate-by-country (accessed 20 February 2025).

Worrell, DeLisle. *Development and Stabilization in Small Open Economies: Theories and Evidence from Caribbean Experience.* Abingdon: Routledge, 2023.

Wright, John. *The Trans-Saharan Slave Trade.* London: Routledge, 2007.

Wrigley, E.A. *Energy and the English Industrial Revolution.* Cambridge: Cambridge University Press, 2015.

INDEX